Walk With Me

Reflections of a Parish Priest

FATHER TIMOTHY HORAN

ISBN 979-8-89130-085-9 (paperback)
ISBN 979-8-88943-972-1 (hardcover)
ISBN 979-8-88943-971-4 (digital)

Christian Faith Publishing
832 Park Avenue
Meadville, PA 16335
www.christianfaithpublishing.com

Printed in the United States of America

CONTENTS

Introduction v

Chapter 1: Me and God 1

Chapter 2: Jesus: God's Son, Our Brother 21

Chapter 3: Being Catholic 33

Chapter 4: Habits and Virtues 47

Chapter 5: Parents and Children 85

Chapter 6: Power of Prayer 105

Chapter 7: Finding Hope: "Dealing with Temptation,
Addiction, and Failure" 117

Chapter 8: Storytelling 127

Chapter 9: Joy and Love 145

INTRODUCTION

These reflections originated as articles in a parish bulletin. They are meant to touch on common thoughts and experiences of life, where the average person may fail to see their deeper meaning or message to us. So walk with me as I share my experiences with you and hopefully help deepen your relationship with God.

Think of a cup of chocolate pudding that cools with that thin skin that forms over the top. These brief reflections try peeling off the skin to get to the pudding. The pudding is God's wisdom hidden in plain sight. God is everywhere trying to break into our lives.

Jesus told parables using everyday life to reveal how God's kingdom works. So too, these reflections use pictures and images (sometimes silly) that can help to "feel and see" the teachings of our faith. They are meant to help strengthen our relationship with God.

Serious students of theology will perhaps roll their eyes at the simple "un-nuanced" messages contained within this book, but I am confident that what you read, though at times incomplete, has a message in concert with Catholic teaching. Common sense combined with Sacred Scripture try to show with a concrete image the logic and sense of what we believe.

There's no special order to these musings, just things I think most people have contemplated from time to time. I've drawn on my priesthood of forty years: hearing confessions, going to hospitals, teaching high school students, marrying, and burying. One thing unifies all of us, we all struggle with life sometimes.

My hope is that one or two of these reflections might provide some guidance and perhaps be a light in a dark time, or something to bring to your prayer and hopefully bring you a smile or two.

CHAPTER 1

Me and God

All of Me

I'm thinking of a spiritual lesson I've had to learn over and over in my life. It's the simple fact that God wants all of me.

What do we mean when we say "all of me" (all of you)? Think of our many parts...our mind and its reasoning, our memory, our desires, our freedom, our work, talents, relationships, etc. God wants us to commit all these things to him.

The problem is I want to be in charge of them. After all...it's *my* life! "But...don't ask me to give you my habits or my preferences. I've spent a lifetime developing them: my bedtime, my cocktail, my personal time, a particular hobby, etc., all these are mine. I'll do what I want with them."

So God is patient. He lets us have our way. Habits and preferences (even the good ones) start to protect themselves. To the point where they can start to run the show. We start living in a way that expects these habits to have no interference. ("What do you mean the plane is delayed? This just can't be. I have to be in Rochester this evening!" *or* "No coffee? That's ridiculous!")

Once again, God lets us have our way. And I don't know about you, but every time I take free rein of my life, with no concern for God's will (I'm a good guy—I don't need God's will to tell me what to do)...things get muddy.

It's weird. I start out wanting a little "life for myself." God won't mind. And now I discover there's a growing part of me that doesn't want God interfering with my habits at all. And look what's happened to God. God becomes "the Law," the cop in my rearview mirror. A killjoy, someone to fear or at least avoid. This, friends, is the effect of original sin in us. God is someone to flee. Poor God. How we twist things about Him. How we make Him out to be some grumpy boss who loves to order people around. Our vision of life slowly changes. Happiness is something to be grasped by ourselves. God is someone to flee. Adam and Eve hid themselves.

So what went wrong? We did. We failed to give God everything. Call it what you want…mistrust, selfishness, pride, arrogance…it's all the same. It's a voice that says, "*Nobody is going to tell me what to do.*" Quietly, God calls to us, but we're not in the mood to listen.

Ever have that feeling? Ever hear yourself saying that? Welcome to this fallen world. We've forgotten that God loves us. We've forgotten that, in His knowing love, He knows us better than we know ourselves. He made us! And it's from this love we receive His will. And get this. God's will is our true happiness! St. Ignatius of Loyola, founder of the Jesuits, prayed this prayer (the Suscipe) for God to have all of him. See what you think.

"Take, O Lord, and receive my entire liberty, my memory, my understanding and my whole will. All that I am and all that I possess, Thou hast given me: I surrender it all to Thee to be disposed of according to Thy will. Give me only Thy love and Thy grace; with these I will be rich enough and will desire nothing more. Amen."

Two Voices: My Spirit and the Holy Spirit

Voices are like fingerprints, each is as unique as the person who speaks with it. You can be walking down a crowded concourse at an airport and hear your brother/sister/friend calling you, and immediately you know it's someone who knows you.

It's not so easy to hear the voice of the Holy Spirit. The reason for this is that he speaks in a whisper. It's a low, brief, quiet speech that we can easily miss if we aren't paying attention. The second reason it can be hard to hear is because it often sounds just like *my* voice. And so sometimes I think I'm hearing God's will for me when really I'm just hearing myself wanting what I want. So how do we tell the difference? Read on!

Every once in a while, you hear deep in your heart "a feeling that has a voice like yours" telling you something you need to hear. It goes like this for me: it starts with a feeling, let's say frustration. "I'm sick and tired of being the one who makes the peace—let someone else get everybody together." This is *my* voice expressing a very familiar frustration with having to put aside my feelings for the sake of the good.

But then I hear way down inside… "Tim" (this voice knows me by name)…and usually a few seconds later… "you know what is needed here, don't you?" Then *my* voice speaks, "Yes. I guess so." Then the Spirit speaks… "Well?"

Something not to be missed is that there are actually *two* graces happening here. The first is the grace to hear the voice of your conscience ("you know what is needed here"). The second is to know the source of what you are hearing—"Hey, this is your conscience speaking to you. Listen up." How can we tell which voice we're hearing, our own or the Holy Spirit? Here are some pointers to hearing God's voice:

- God's voice usually invites us to put ourselves second to someone or something that needs help.
- When we hear the voice of the Holy Spirit, there is a feeling of "being reminded of something we already know deep in our heart."
- God's voice carries with it a personal note. What I'm hearing has a feeling of "being meant for me" at this time, in this place.
- God's voice is persistent. It keeps coming back even when we may flee. It can feel like it is pursuing us.
- If what we are about to do (or have done) is good and virtuous, God's voice is usually quiet and peaceful. "Good," it says. If, however, we are contemplating something sin-

ful, the voice is generally loud and insistent. "Stop this!" or "No. This is wrong!"

- God's voice generally asks me to "surrender" to "give in." It must have been what Jesus heard in the garden that night, "Not my will, Lord, but Thine be done."
- There is generally a peace that comes over us that tells us what we're hearing or feeling comes from a place (person) that loves us and speaks goodness to us.

So, Lord, give us the ears to hear your voice deep in our hearts.

God: Coweaver of Our Life

Something happened a few years back at a conference I was attending. The subject was vocation and how we find God's way and plan for our life. A young priest presented an image that surprised and delighted all of us. He gave us a picture of how life gets pieced together in partnership with God. He used this image. See what you think.

Picture you're weaving a cloth with various shuttles and several colored yarns attached to them. The cloth is suspended over your head much like an umbrella. The garment you're weaving is, of course, "your life." But remember, you can only see it from underneath. The finished cloth can only be seen from above. As you view your cloth from the bottom, you see several openings which could receive your shuttle. So seeing the pattern you've already begun, you choose an opening that seems to best add to your plan. You push the shuttle through and wait for its return.

Meanwhile, God is there above to receive your choice. He takes his time in returning the shuttle. He's been waiting for you to make your choice since He's partnering with you as coweaver! Finally, He drops the shuttle back down to you, but not exactly where you thought He would. It's "over there." "Oh," we think. "That changes things. Now what? Where do I send my shuttle back to Him?" And up and down, the shuttle of life goes. Each time, we make the best judgment we can about life's choices… Is this the person I should marry? Do I work or stay home with the children? Do I apply for the new opening at work? Where do we send the children to school? How do I handle this new problem? etc.

So you think about things, maybe talk things over with family or a friend. Hopefully, you'll say a prayer for the Holy Spirit to guide you. But then comes the moment of decision ("Mom, Dad, I've decided to go into the military."), and with that, you've sent the shuttle up through the cloth of your life. What will God send back? We'll see… Get the picture? It's really a nice meditation on the partnership God has with us in guiding us through our lives.

Two points seem critical to me in this process:

1. When we ponder where to send up our choices (the shuttle), there needs to be some sort of prayer. "Lord, guide me, enlighten me. Show me your will. I give it to you." Then… do your best. God will guide this whole process. He loves you!

2. When God drops the shuttle back down to you (in other words, when life gives its unforeseen events), we can receive this as God's answer, whatever it might be. This is an act of faith in its rawest form. Your feelings may not be brimming with confidence. That's okay. Faith helps us submit. "I don't get it, Lord, but I trust in you."

Remember, we only see our life from below. God, our coweaver, sees the big picture. God knows stuff about your life that you don't. Do you trust Him to help you create the tapestry of your life?

God's providence (His guiding grace) extends even to our bad choices (decisions made thoughtlessly or in emotional turmoil). God can work with our mistakes—if we turn things over to Him. God is waiting for your next prayer as together you weave the pattern of your life. Partner with God. Make your garment breathtaking!

God Doesn't Need You. He Wants You

I'd like to share with you something a wise old priest told me some forty years ago. It changed my life. It can change anyone's. First, you need to know the turmoil I was in as I contemplated whether or not I could live life as a priest. Back and forth I went, sometimes I felt confident and excited about this way of life. Other times (equal in frequency), I felt overwhelmed by my selfishness and ability to find fault with everything and everybody. How could I possibly be a priest with such an attitude?

So all tied up in knots, I went to my friend Fr. Francis. "Father," I said, "I don't know if I can do this (priesthood). But I don't want to let God down. If I leave, maybe God will be upset with me."

Fr. Francis laughed. "Tim, do you think God needs you? God will accomplish his will either with you or without you. Nothing can keep God from finishing what he's started. Bottom line… God doesn't need you, Tim."

I was shocked. "You mean I'm free to leave? God won't be mad at me?"

"Yes, you're free to leave. He won't be mad."

I can't describe the huge weight that lifted off my shoulders at that moment. Suddenly, it became clear what God was doing. He was offering an invitation. And it was just that…an invitation, a gift. Did I have to accept it? No. Would there be other gifts and invitations? Yes. Could I choose another way of life that would be pleasing to God? Of course. That's the way God is. He never gives up on us. Never takes his ball and goes home. Ah, but God knows our deepest happiness and has a grace (gift) prepared to offer us if we want to say "yes."

So let's talk about you. What is God offering you to participate in? The answer most times comes in looking at the "here and now." What's your situation? Married? Children? Student? Single? Sad? Feeling blessed? Need money? Worried? Whatever and wherever you find yourself—there is God's Spirit. In each of these situations, there is work to be done. This present moment contains an invitation to cooperate with God in bringing goodness (Christ) to the world.

We can wish we were somewhere else. Perhaps it was our thoughtlessness or selfishness that got us where we are. In the end, it doesn't matter. What matters is "right now." God is with you. What do you feel called to do with God's help?

And it's in saying "yes" to God and his invitation that we discover a "lightness" to God's will. A new purpose suddenly appears where before there was confusion, frustration, sadness. "Learn from me for I am meek and humble of heart. And you will find rest...for my yoke is easy, my burden light" (Mt. 11:30).

Try to see the invitation God gives us to partner with Him. Remember. It's an invitation. God doesn't need you, silly. He *wants* you.

"Lord, here I am. You know I'd be in a better place if I'd only listened to you. But that doesn't matter now. What matters is that, with your help, I start to do what you've put into my heart to do. You've been there all along, haven't you? But now, Lord, I see. And now I want to do things your way. Please help me."

Have You Eaten? (God Our Food)

Do you ever get going during a busy day and forget to eat at the proper time? Maybe it's 3:00 p.m., and suddenly you feel the bottom drop out. No energy, listless, irritable, maybe even a little depressed. It feels like life turns grey and impossible. So...get something to eat! That's right, most problems in life can be dealt with if we've had sufficient food. The world is a brighter place when good food is in your system.

Angels don't have this problem of finding food for strength. They have no bodies. Being pure spirit means you don't have to stop your angelic praising to sit for a meal. (It also means they don't have the sloppy pleasure of a cheeseburger and fries! Poor angels.) God has made us humans in such a way that we must pause two or three times a day to take nourishment for our bodies. What a launching pad for God to visit us!

Jesus chose the human experience of taking food to be the way he would come to us down through history. In the context of the ancient Jewish Passover (the meal of roasted lamb, commemorating the night God freed the Jews from slavery in Egypt), Jesus saw himself to be the "New Lamb" whose body and blood would bring life to those who receive it.

He began to teach his disciples this insight about who he was and what he must do for those who believe in him. "I am the living bread come down from heaven. Unlike your ancestors who ate (the manna in the desert) whoever eats this bread (my body) will live forever" (John 6:58).

Like the lamb that was slain at Passover, this new meal would require the death of Jesus, "the Lamb of God." So the night before his death, gathered with the apostles, "he took the bread, said the blessing," and said, "This is my body" and over the cup "this is…my blood poured out for you." Now eat and drink.

So that's it gang. A new food for humanity—Jesus's body and blood. The first hearers of this message were totally grossed out. "How can he say he will give us his flesh to eat?" And "because of this many followers turned back and would not go with him anymore" (Jn. 6:67).

So what about you? Can you see God's plan to get inside us with His Son? Does the image of the innocent lamb speak to you? Be aware that it takes years of eating to build a body—so too, to become a Christian. Does the change from bread to "my flesh" bother you? Don't you think that if God could come up with the idea of your little daughter and give her your smile—he could change bread into anything he wants?

None of us knows "how" the bread becomes Jesus's body (we say of course "by the Holy Spirit," which is Bible talk for "He will do it.") He said so. Theologians call it transubstantiation. What we do know is God created each of us. (We didn't) And we experience a restless hunger to live in a state of being that is truth, love, and joy (eternal life). What we know is that no one has ever gone so deeply into the human condition… "like us in all things but sin." He shows us what causes us to be far from God (sin and selfishness). And he lays his life down in such a way that he becomes our food to bring us to God who won't rest till we are all one in the Body of Christ.

Perhaps a little prayer here… "Dear God and Father, help me trust your divine word which came to us in Christ Jesus. And trusting that he would not trick us, let me receive his body and blood in humble faith. Let this heavenly food transform me into a person worthy to be called Christian."

I asked little Valery (preparing to receive her first Holy Communion), "Valery, why do you believe that this little piece of flat bread becomes Jesus as food?"

"Because He said so" was her answer.

That's faith in the raw.

God's Kingdom: Here and Now, but Not Yet

Jesus preaches his first public sermon in the gospel (Matthew 5). He says open your eyes, change your lives for "the Kingdom of God is at hand." To paraphrase a bit, Jesus might have added, "What you've been looking for from God…what humans have longed for since the beginning of time is here." The reign of God's kingdom is happening now. Look around.

And where do we see it? When it first dawned on the earth, it appeared in Bethlehem. Jesus is the beginning of the Kingdom of God. In his mind and heart, we have the thoughts and desires of God for humankind. We hear this echoed later in the gospel when Philip the apostle asked Jesus to "show us the Father" in heaven.

"Philip," Jesus said, "I've been with you this long and you do not know the Father? Do you not know that when you see me you see the Father?" (Jn. 14:9). So the Kingdom of God has already started in the one person of Jesus.

I keep thinking of those events of 1967 when Neil Armstrong stepped on the moon. "The Eagle has landed!" announced the jubilant voice. And then the first human stepped there. The moon now is forever ours. We stepped there, we planted our flag there, and we even hit golf balls there! The reign of humankind has begun on the moon.

But Jesus, as we know, has ascended into heaven. We can't see him like Philip could. So is the Kingdom still here? And if so, where?

Jesus told us how to find it. "The Kingdom of God does not come in such a way as to be seen. No one will say here it is! Or there it is! because the Kingdom of God is *within you*" (Lk 17:20). It is born in us in baptism; a seed (like the mustard seed) which grows of its own accord to enormous size. It brings the beginning of eternal life to those who receive it. Watch for Jesus's parables in this context. "The Kingdom of Heaven is like…" He has to give us pictures because it's hard to put the nature of the Kingdom into words. Why? Because it is a spiritual reality, one that must be perceived by faith. "Thomas you believe because you have seen (the nail marks), blessed are those who have not seen and yet believe" (Jn. 20:24).

So where do I find God's Kingdom today? Any act that brings God's goodness to the world has its roots in the kingdom. "When did we see you hungry and feed you? As often as you did it to the least of my brethren, you did it for me"… Welcome to my Kingdom.

If You Were God

If you were God and you chose to be born a human being, how would you have done it? Find a list of choices below and see how your preferences compare with God's. (Remember, you are God; the whole world is yours.)

1. When would you come to earth? Probably around this time, right? At least a time in history with electricity and light and indoor plumbing and TV, of course! Guess what? God came two thousand years ago not long after the Bronze Age. People were just learning farming and writing.
2. Where would you be born? Let's see… Paris? New York? Hawaii? Some exotic and beautiful place probably. Guess what? God was born in a backward little town called Bethlehem next to the largest desert in the world.
3. Who would be your family? Your blood? Some famous stock of Roman or Greek or Egyptian nobility? Guess what? Your blood is Jewish, a minor tribal grouping of people who were slaves for most of their history.

4. What would your financial situation be? I mean really… God is rich. Right? God, as man, would have the material world at his fingertips. What comfort would not be yours while on earth? Guess what? He was born in a stable. His parents had to stretch to make the simplest of payments. The Bible says he literally had no home.

5. Who would your friends and associates be? The educated, the executives, the cultured and high class, the religious for sure. Guess what? He hung with the working class. Fishermen, carpenters. He ate with the outcasts: extortionists (tax collectors), prostitutes, lepers.

6. Who would you have close to you? Your wife? Your cabinet? Cleopatra? The queen of Sheba? The Harvard board of directors? Guess what? You never marry ("What's wrong with that, boy?"). Your board of directors prove to be traitors and cowards.

7. What would be your greatest achievement? To be universally acclaimed as king of all the world? To have every people and nation bow to your smallest command? Guess what? Your greatest achievement will be your death—naked and nailed to a cross—and then your resurrection.

I think you begin to see how differently God chose to live his life from the way you and I would. That's because we don't get it. We think the purpose of life is to enjoy, to be fulfilled, to be happy in the ways this world can deliver. And as lovely as they are, we must be careful. We can get blinded by the shiny, sparkly things and begin to think that having them is why I'm here on earth.

To correct this, Jesus came to show us what God the Father had in mind when he made us humans. How we are to be a light to the world, not a sponge. We are a seed that dies to itself so it can give life a hundredfold. We are a branch united to God's vine (Christ) that receives his very life into us. (Read Mt. 5:13—The Beatitudes for the new key to happiness.)

And here's the point…if we miss this, we miss everything… "apart from me you can do nothing" (Jn. 15:5). Like a branch separated from the vine, we wither over time. That's because we're living life apart from our source—God. What wondrous love God is! The small, the humble, the gentle reveal His infinite power. This power of love has overcome the world (Jn. 16:33).

Thoughtless Beauty

There's a crab apple tree outside my office window. I'd say it's fifteen to twenty years old. Each spring, it explodes into a wonderful cloud of pink blossoms that last for about ten days. It stands bare right now except for several thousand little crab apples arranged throughout its skinny tree limbs. They'll all be eaten by hungry robins come spring. And here, friends, hangs our lesson for the week.

Against the dull gray sky, the tree is all in black silhouette. Each little crab apple hangs at random, like a droplet along each branch. The whole tree fits exactly in my window as if it were a picture frame. It's perfect. And that's the point. The tree just happened. There wasn't a care in the world when each apple began to grow on the tree, yet it has a balance and proportion any artist would covet. You could entitle the art of my window view… "Crab Apple against a Winter Sky."

I'm sure you've seen this "thoughtless beauty" of nature for yourself. Walk through a pine forest. Look down at the random pine needles on the ground. They are perfectly, beautifully fallen. See the perfect curve of the snow drift at the corner of your house. (How did the wind get to be such an artist?) I won't even start with the random beauty of clouds or sunlight. The point is…it is exquisite. And it's free for any eye that wishes to really look. Listen to the leaves in the wind, waves on the beach, thunder in the storm…they're perfect in a wondrous way. And it all happens with a carelessness that would make any artist, who sweats and strains to create, jealous of the brilliance it displays.

And guess what? It's *for you*. God made it for you, not for any other creature. Do you think the deer in the forest gives a fig for the brilliant fall leaves that surround it? Does the eagle pause in midflight to marvel at the beauty in the valley below? Do the flames dancing in your fireplace giving calm and comfort mean anything to your cat?

When you think about it, we humans are the spokespersons for the rest of creation. We have a voice to speak on behalf of the running stream, the soaring eagle… "Thank you, Lord."

Pope Francis has written an encyclical called *Laudato Si* ("Praise be to You"). In it, he points to an appreciation of this created world as a gift of God. He reminds us that the earth is humanity's common home; it needs our care and protection in the way we use its natural resources. The generations to come have an equal right to drink clean water and breathe clean air.

But back to us humans for a moment. Of all the beauty of God's creation (the birds, the flowers, and yes, those little puppies), can you think of anything quite as captivating, and endlessly expressive, as the human face? Why is that? Because it is the window to the human spirit…which, in case you'd forgotten, is a face that God had. To look at the human face is to see some faint image of God himself. All this is to say, "Oh Lord, how great thou art."

Open your eyes. His glory is everywhere.

"Lord, Is That You?"

So there they were, four miles out into the sea. It was about 3:00 a.m. ("the fourth watch of the night"), and they hit a storm. Wind and waves were so strong as to make the apostles fear that they might drown.

I can't think of a more frightening way to die. I learned to swim when I was about eight or nine years old, but I've never been very good at it. The swim instructor would tell us, "Relax, the water will hold you up. Don't fight the water, it will only tire you out." I never could trust this, and so any time I'm in water over my head, I'm pretty anxious.

The apostles were fishermen. We can presume they had seen their share of stormy seas. But tonight was different…fear gripped them all. Adding to the terror was the strange figure of a man walking on the water toward them. "A ghost," they thought. Surely, tonight we die. So the apostles "cried out in fear."

I don't know about you, but I would be just as scared as they were. Life sometimes resembles that stormy night. Our life is tossed about by many things…sickness, a runaway child, a lost job, a broken relationship, a freak accident. All seems lost. We cry out in fear. Then something happens. Peter calls out, "Is that you, Lord? Call for me to come to you." "Come." He hears. Now here's the part that really gets me. In spite of all that's happening around him…the huge waves splashing over the boat, the howling wind, and screaming apostles… he gets out of the boat! Oh, Peter. "No! You'll drown!" Are you nuts?

What was he thinking, this rough and impetuous fisherman? It seems to have been a blind act of *trust*. A trust that the voice he heard was his friend telling him not to be afraid, "Take courage. It is I." Now where do you think this amazing act of trust came from? Do you think Peter just sort of summoned it up out of his human heart? (Remember, he was the one who, when confronted by the little servant girl, denied he ever knew Jesus.) Do you think it was deep inside him just waiting for such a moment to show his great courage and faith? I don't think so. It was a moment of grace. "A free and unmerited favor of God," says the *Catholic Encyclopedia*, "given to empower a person to act for goodness."

Somehow, Peter was touched beyond his natural fear at that moment to turn to his Lord in faith. And lo! He began to walk on the water toward Christ (his faith would falter a moment later, of course, when he looked back to the waves around him and, in doing so, took his eyes off the one he trusted). But here's the point. The grace to trust that the Lord is with you is a favor that God promises us (it's on every page of the New Testament—but, like Peter, we must call out, "Lord, is that you?").

"Help me, Lord. I believe, help my unbelief." These are wonderful prayers. Now trust…not in your goodness, but in God's goodness to you.

O Lord, my boat is so small, and your ocean is so big…

My God, How Great Thou Art

I think one of the chief reasons people have difficulty in hearing the gospel message about God is the "upstairs-downstairs" image of God in heaven and we humans on earth. It just doesn't describe the universe as we experience it in the modern world. The Bible image of God showed him "up" in heaven looking "down" on us. The rains fell from the heavens at his command. Somewhere, there was a "throne" on which God sat while a "choir of angels" sang his praises.

Copernicus (1473–1543) sent the religious world reeling when he discovered the sun, not the earth, as the center of our solar system. Galileo, a century later, proved those same findings in spite of vigorous Church protests.

All kinds of things got shaken up. The immense size of the universe, seen through that new gizmo (the telescope), threw out the notion of "up" or "down." Later still, Charles Darwin proposed a new law of nature—the evolution of the species (including humans!). The Garden of Paradise (seen as a real garden somewhere in the Middle East), where Adam and Eve lived an idyllic life, was now consigned to "religious myth."

It's not so much the modern mind finds the existence of a Supreme Being unreasonable; rather, it's the image of God living much like an earthly king in a penthouse high above the created world that can make many reject religion. What is needed is a new way to imagine the unfathomable mystery of the divine. Theology is working to find new ways to (1) articulate the truths already revealed about God and humanity in the Bible and (2) develop a way of talking about God where the actual findings of science can help us to better speak of God to the modern mind.

One of the chief insights of the last eighty years has been to see God as "participating" in the story of an unfolding, still-evolving creation. Teilhard de Chardin S.J. proposes we see God as the love that pours itself out as it pushes creation to its fulfillment.

Consider what has happened over these seventeen billion years of the universe. We've gone from the primitive elements of matter combining in ever greater complexity to the appearance of living beings! These living beings become the evermore complex life of plants and (billions of years later) animals. From this animal life—don't get nervous here, this is wonderful!—comes intelligent life (humanity). Life can now begin to understand itself! The power "to know" coming from dust, just incredible!

And then from the ability to know, there comes the ability to love. Over these billions of years, creation has learned how to love. Where does the universe give evidence of love? In the human being ("And God said, let us make man in our image and likeness. In the divine image he made him" [Gen. 2].). No other creature loves its young for their entire lives. Buries their dead. Cries tears of tenderness, sacrifices for the poor, celebrates birthdays, makes dolls for children to play with. If you're a creature from outer space and you're looking for this amazing occurrence called *love*…you'll have to visit the human beings.

So what now? Where is God? What's he waiting for? "In the fullness of time, God sent his only son. He came as the son of a human mother…so that we might become God's children" (Galatians 4:4). Jesus is God's full entrance into the long story of creation and life. God is not sitting on a throne in the penthouse of heaven; he is the power of love working through the process of evolution. Jesus is God's love made visible. The human person leads creation back to God.

But the job is not done. God's love continues through nature and human history to bring all creation into its divine fullness. That's "when everything is placed under Christ's rule, then the Son himself will place himself under God: and God will then be all in all" (1 Corinthians 15:24–28—read the whole passage. Amazing!).

What a long and breathtaking story. God is love beyond all telling, and he's chosen to show himself in the love of Christ…in which we have a share and, by God's grace, are invited into the divine Body of Christ.

Dear God…how great thou art.

God... No God-Important Consequences

Just west of De Moines, Iowa, Interstate 80 hits a fork in the road. If you're going to San Francisco, you keep on I-80 heading west. If you want to go to Houston, you bear south on I-35. Two roads heading in two different directions. Where do you want to go?

It's like life. Where you want to go determines which road you take. Most times, our choices are day-to-day and have to do with groceries or family gatherings or what's on TV. Seldom do we think of the big picture. (Where *am* I going with my life?) Two roads lie ahead of us. One directs our lives to God. Do you want to meet Him in heaven? The other road is in search of some happiness here on earth before the lights get turned off.

The God factor is critical in how you experience life. Things go off in two very different directions depending on what you believe about God and whether this God has a purpose for your life. See what you think... Here's what happens if there is no God (or if there's no way of knowing anything about him anyway).

1. Nothing means anything. "Good" or "bad" is merely your opinion. What you think is "your truth." What I think is "my truth." In fact, there is no ultimate truth.
2. Since there is no ultimate goodness to guide our actions, then "lesser gods" will serve. Money, possessions, leisure, and pleasure are what life is about.
3. Might makes right. My wanting more makes me a potential threat to what you have. (Why can't I take what you have? You say, "That's not right!" I say, "Says who!")
4. Sickness, poverty, or tragic happenings can only be seen as absurd or real bad luck. Flee these things. Pity those who encounter them. They are the "unlucky ones."
5. Any moment of beauty or longing that our lives have ultimate meaning is an illusion and should be tolerated like Santa Claus with our children. (Let this God myth continue as long as it keeps people happy.)

6. An "eye for an eye and a tooth for a tooth" is the best way of dealing with human conflict. But who has the authority to declare something as righteous or criminal?
7. Our best hopes for our children would be that they were skillful hunters in getting what they want in a world that doesn't care.
8. About the best thing we can wish anybody is "good luck."

Pretty grim, wouldn't you say? Yet that is the way of the human heart without God. You see, we humans were *made for* God. Made to enter into a relationship with Him, and without Him...we lose our purpose for existing. We become, as the great theologian Romano Guardini put it, "clever animals."

The revealed God of Christianity changes everything. Here's what happens when you let God into your life (these contrast with 1–8 above):

1. Everything means something. The fact that something "is" gives it purpose in the plan of God. All that exists shares to some degree with the truth of its maker.
2. The "lesser goods" become what they were intended to be—joys in life that point to a loving God who wishes our happiness. They are not an end in themselves.
3. By God's love (revealed in Christ), we become brothers and sisters to each other, *not* "threats" or rivals.
4. The hard things in life (sickness, etc.) have been redeemed. They too now serve God's purpose. They reveal true love. (We only know this by Jesus Christ who took suffering and death to himself to reveal what God's love is like.) "Love bears all things" (1 Cor. 13).
5. Longing for peace or purpose in life is a grace put there by God to remind us of our true home. "Our hearts are restless until they rest in thee, oh Lord" (St. Augustine).
6. "We hold these truths to be self-evident, all men are created equal and endowed by their Creator..."

7. Our best hope for our children is that they would grow to be good and kind and happy in "doing what is right and just." And that they, too, would come to know the presence of God in their life.
8. Our best wish for someone? "Go with God."

Go with God.

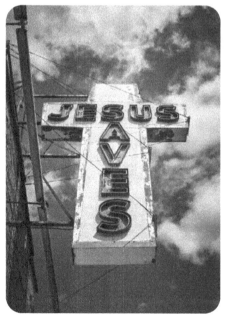

CHAPTER 2

Jesus: God's Son, Our Brother

"It is good that I go away…"

Recently, we celebrated the feast of the Ascension. We heard how Jesus gathered his disciples one last time to tell them to go out into the world and proclaim his message. And then he went away. He left the world. He's back in heaven. In fact, Jesus said it was better for us if he left.

How can that be? It sort of makes us feel like orphans, doesn't it? "Jesus, we were just getting the hang of it, just starting to understand. You had to die in fulfillment of God's will so that you would then be raised from the dead. Truly, you are the Son of God. We get it. But now you're leaving us. Stay with us, Lord. Give us your voice to hear. Show us what we must do each day. Lead us into victory, Lord. Perform miracles…cure cancer, prevent global warming, feed the starving, put an end to war, bring freedom to all people. Don't go, Lord, we need you here!"

So how is it better that Jesus leaves us? May I suggest a couple of reasons?

1. So we might participate in his mission as equal partners. Jesus calls us his friends, not his children. And as good friends, he entrusts himself to us to represent him in the world. If he remained physically here with us, he'd do all the

work. We'd be calling on him to do all the problem-solving. He wants us to be coworkers, esteemed colleagues.

2.   His light would shine so brightly as to obscure the light we all carry in us by virtue of our own baptism. The world would only listen to him, not to you or me or the pope or anybody. We'd all sort of disappear.

3.   He desires that we each come to full stature, mature in the faith; ready to offer our lives, not as children, but as loving, self-directed adults…our own person, in love with God. It's like a child who has to move away from his father to discover who he is. Jesus wants us to discover who we are. So he goes away.

4.   If he didn't go away, then the Holy Spirit wouldn't come. Why? Because the Holy Spirit is "the Voice of Christ" given to each of us to guide and strengthen and teach. We wouldn't heed that voice in us if all we had to do is turn on the Jesus Channel to see him on TV.

5.   If he were still here physically, then when he was in Rome, he couldn't be in Rochester! But now that the Holy Spirit is here, Jesus can be with all of the believers—personally.

"So it is good for you that I go," says the Lord. (John 16:7). And now…comes the Holy Spirit!

What Child Is This

In my youth I thought it would all work out. This world would get it together. Good people, working together for the common good, would make this world a happy place. If we just put our minds to it, we can solve the problems that cause so much pain in the world. Hunger, poverty, hatred…are all fixable if we just work together.

I don't believe that anymore. Even on our best days, there's just something in the human condition that causes us to go off the rail. This dark pull causes many to turn to an anxious life of getting and protecting what they can. A suspicion about people's motives keeps us from trusting each other. And on and on.

But something outrageous has happened. Someone has come into the world to show us how to fix the downward spiral of selfishness. God, who is love, has come to make "all things new." There is in the human heart a self-inflicted wound that brings fear, greed, and other nasty things. But the remedy God provides is beyond our wildest expectations.

The short of it is, God gives us a new heart…a heart like His. How will this happen? (Here's the mind-boggling part.) God became a human being. God took a human heart. (God's human heart…think of it!) Born of Mary, his human name is Jesus. He has the only remedy deep enough and true enough to break the chains of selfishness that grips the world. How will Jesus show us this life-changing love? (Get ready. This is the part that's hard to understand.) He will have to die. Why does he have to die? Because love can only "love to the end." And by dying, sin has finally met its match—a love that is willing to die at the hand of the hater for the purpose of revealing the love of God for humanity.

St. Paul tells us, He "became sin for us. He who knew no sin" (2 Cor. 5:21). And he took all that sin can do and *kissed it!* Taking it in his loving arms down with him when he died. "Father, forgive them, they know not what they do" (Lk. 23:34). Sin and death died in Christ. It's a kind of love never seen before.

God's not done. He will raise this noble heart of Jesus to a new life in the Resurrection. And here's where we get a new heart. We now are reborn by the grace of God. By adoption, we become Children of God and begin a new life "in Christ" seeking to live as Christ lived. This changes everything. There is something really new here. Now there is hope. Hope that with Christ (*only* with Christ— we've tried everything else!)…with Christ, we are reconciled to one another since we have all been loved and saved by Christ who kissed us in our sin. He lives in you. He lives in me. We are brothers and sisters in Christ who has loved us all. Let's let the world know.

"When you see me, you see the Father."

Certainly, you've watched young families, parents, and children shopping or going to church or in a restaurant. Sometimes it's hard to see the physical resemblance between parent and child. The hair or eyes or coloring don't seem to match. (Must be the mailman! The joke goes) But more often than not, the children bear a striking resemblance to one or both of the parents. My sisters have many of my father's features while it's easy to see I'm my mother's child. I think it's safe to say Jesus (who received his body from Mary, not Joseph) must have looked just like her. Who do you most resemble?

Anyway, in the gospel, Philip the Apostle, seemingly frustrated with Jesus's constant reference to his Father, blurts out "show us the father and that will explain everything" (John 14:8–18). This brings an amazing statement from Jesus. "Philip, you've been with me all this time and you still do not know me? When you see me, you see the Father."

Something very important is being revealed to us here. Jesus is saying, "Do you want to enter the Kingdom of God, and there possess eternal life? Do you want to meet my Father from whom I draw my life? Do you want to find the source of all goodness, love, and truth?" "Then believe me. I am the way to the Father. No one comes to the Father except through me. The Father is in me and I in him" (John 14:1–12).

There you have it, friends. In a nutshell…if we want to know who God is and what he is like, follow Jesus Christ. He is the visible, human expression of God his Father. So every word he speaks in the gospels, every time he touches someone sick or tormented, every time he cries out on our behalf…this is God leading us to God. "Believe me…that I am in the Father and the Father is in me. Or (if that doesn't move you) believe because of the works I do."

What moves you? His teaching (love thy enemy), his care for the poor, his love for the sinner and lost sheep, his constant welcome to all ("Come to me all you who are heavy burdened"). And most amazing was laying his life out on the cross in an act of fidelity to his Father's command ("The Father who dwells in me is doing his works" [v. 10]). This was the way it had to be in order to show the Father's divine love for us.

So I guess the question is—do you believe this? Just a simple "yes, Lord" way deep in our heart. "Yes, Lord. I believe."

Do I understand how and why all this happened? No. Do I perfectly obey his words and instructions? Nope. Do I always remember to pray and give thanks to God for his Son? No. Do I always resist the very things that I know are against God's will? No, but... I just believe. I see signs all around me that Jesus is alive. I see him in people who try to fail and try again (and keep trying; Jesus fell three times). I see him in women and men who daily spend their lives giving to others. I see him in the refugees waiting in food lines far, far from their homes. I see him in people who do the right thing in spite of ridicule and taunting.

There are too many wonderful things in this world because of him and what he did for me to not believe. Now it's time to give back. It's time to "follow." It's time to stop being afraid of everything, and holding on to everything. Because he said, "I will come back and take you to myself. So that where I am you also may be."

Lord, we believe. Help our unbelief.

My Friend Jesus. Is It Possible?

I recently attended a funeral for a previous college professor of mine. Fr. Robert Madden taught English literature to generations of students and was well-known for his knowledge, wit, and kindly way. Perhaps greatest of his gifts, as noted at the funeral, was his ability to be a true friend. Students and faculty alike would turn to Bob for advice, encouragement, and his delightful company. Fr. Madden had no short memory. A brief undergraduate stay has led many to a life-long friendship with him. Bob knew you and had a personal interest in how your life was going.

It got me thinking how it might be that same way with Jesus. Why should Christ be any less of a friend? (He calls himself that, by the way (Jn. 15:15). Is it possible to have a personal friendship with Jesus? If so, how does one go about getting it/experiencing it?

Let's use Fr. Madden as an example. I had heard about this short, round, red-faced professor from all the upper class students. I knew he was a good lecturer, a master of his subject, and perhaps best of all, very funny. I heard how he was a demanding grader for both essays and tests. And I heard how he was always ready to help any struggling student in his class. I knew all these things "about" Madden. I was so envious of those who had him in class and could call him by name and hear back theirs. Madden was a "figure" about whom I knew much but someone I'd never met. That was about to end as I began his American literature class my sophomore year. It was there that I learned firs-hand about him. I finally met the man.

Isn't this like Jesus for so many of us? We've heard the Bible stories, we've gotten a picture of him in beard and sandals. We say the prayer He told us to pray. But we've never met Him personally, heard His voice, or felt his presence. Is it possible? Can we really meet Him? The answer is…yes!

But how? Our faith teaches He's "in the Spirit." We can't see or hear Him in the normal everyday way we meet others. We need a new way of seeing and hearing. Empowered by faith in the Resurrection and driven forward by a hunger to know Him, there is a gradual growth in the experience of Jesus present in our lives as friend and Savior.

Where to look to find your friend Jesus:

1. Look closely at the movements of your heart. Moments of love, compassion, sorrow, joy (sometimes accompanied by tears) are signs that Jesus is near. Speak to him at such times. "I am sent to heal the broken hearted" (Lk. 4:18).
2. Pray! "Lord Jesus, let me see you in my life." And then remember that you've prayed for that! God will answer your prayers in some way through the course of the day or week. Generally, it happens through events around you.
3. Watch for "a double grace." The grace of the moment… and…the grace to know "it is the Lord!"
4. Watch God's "little ones." Those especially close to Christ: children, the lost, the poor, the mournful and suffering. They have the spiritual presence of Christ all around them.
5. Pray just one thing for a while… Let me see you, Lord, or show me you are with me.
6. The Eucharist, of course, brings special graces to know Jesus in the "breaking of the bread." It's called asking. And

Jesus says, "Ask and you shall receive. Seek and you shall find" (Mt. 7:7).

Candyland

I'm sure you know people (good people) who have opted to leave organized religion or see the teachings of the Church as irrelevant. "I believe in God, just not all the things we read in the Bible or is taught in church. Science is my guide to what's real in the universe. God is a spiritual feeling no one can explain."

Reflecting on God and science, it seems they describe two different worlds. The world of science and nature is the one that roots us in our daily lives. Religion, on the other hand, is about a world we cannot see. When discussing religion, we often feel our knowledge of this world (astronomy and physics, for example) gets placed on the shelf. Religion describes a different world. For example, the creed says Jesus "came down from heaven," "he suffered death and was buried…and rose again," then he "ascended into heaven," and "is seated at the right hand of the Father."

The words seem to indicate a heaven situated a few miles above us, from which he "came down" and then "ascended" back. It's like a palace in the air with two chairs set side by side. This is heaven. Add to this, Jesus saying, "In my Father's house there are many mansions… I am going to prepare a place for you" (Jn. 14:2), and one can imagine a place not unlike Candyland. There's the Candy Castle, and there on his throne is King Candy.

I'm not trying to be a smart aleck here. This is what the words of the Bible can cause us to imagine about God and Jesus and heaven. And these imaginings can seem childish next to the hard and scary facts about the limitless cosmos. Many rightfully reject the Candy Castle religion and see religion as irrelevant, trusting their own instincts to show them the way.

What can we say to help here? I think the first thing to remember is the difference between believing and imagining. "I believe in God the Father Almighty maker of heaven and earth." This is a statement of faith…there is one God, and all that is comes from God. But then we imagine. "What did making the earth look like?" Michelangelo tried his brilliant best in the Sistine Chapel. Remember that painting of God the Father on the cloud reaching out with his divine finger to touch the finger of the sleeping Adam? Did it really look like that? No. But does it convey a truth? Of course. God created us.

Or the story of Adam and Eve, the serpent and the apple. Did the "fall of humanity" look like that? No. But is it true? Yes, there was a moment, when, by the actions of the first human couple, we have become strangers to God and to ourselves (read St. Paul's Letter to the Romans 7). Think about it the next time you feel life is some huge accident or you are anxious to lock your door at night.

The *what?*… God the eternal has come into our world from outside time and space to become one with the human race in the man Jesus.

The *imagining?*…the Nativity scene or most any Christmas card.

The church wants us to know what is true, then artists and poets imagine the visuals. Some are helpful and inspiring. Some are silly and wrong. There's lot more to talk about here. Another time perhaps.

Jesus: "What do you want me to do for You?"

"The man has been blind for years" (Mark 10). This little conversation in the gospel challenges us to know what we really need in our life. The man is blind, so when asked what kind of help he needed, he was quick to respond… "I want to see!"

Put yourself in the gospel story (Mark 10:46–52). You are the blind person. Jesus is here. You call out. He asks, "What do you want?" And your answer? "Lord, I want…" What? Not so, easy is it? We have to dig deep to discover just what is the desire of our souls. Take some time with this one. It's all very personal, of course, but here are some thoughts as to what one might consider:

- Freedom from whatever keeps you chained to harmful habits and ways of treating people. Freedom from fear, resentment, greed, lust, anger. What keeps you in chains?

- An ability to love again in the face of past disappointments, betrayal, tragedy.
- A personal experience that will let me know that God loves me, and I can give my life to His care.
- A powerful life-changing help for someone I love. Something that lets them see the light and turn from the darkness.
- A personal faith that doesn't turn away from the problems of human history, but one that never despairs of the final victory of God and the salvation of the human race.
- The children. The children. Protect them Lord.
- A grace to hold on to hope in the face of personal loss and sadness.
- That every single human being, born and unborn, go to heaven.

Okay. So we ask the Lord these things or something similar. Now what? Two things happen, I think. First, Jesus has shown you what you *really* want. You experience your heart of hearts, and that's where God is! Stay with this.

Secondly, all our other "wants" take their proper, lesser order. We see them in a new perspective. They don't have the control over us they once had; we're in touch with something bigger and more important—what God wants in us.

Jesus. He's One of Us

Something quite wonderful has happened in the world of theology these past fifty years. Just prior to Vatican II (1958–65), some German theologians were working on a new way of explaining who Jesus is and how he achieved the salvation of the human race. It keeps the traditional doctrine of Christ, of course, but adds a new dimension—from below.

Most notable in this regard was a theologian named Karl Rahner who, in his *Foundations of Christian Faith*, proposed an "ascending

Christology" which would complement the traditional "descending Christology" of the Catholic Church.

The traditional way of viewing Jesus is as the Eternal Word. From all eternity, he has existed with the Father and the Holy Spirit. "True God from True God. Consubstantial with the Father," we recite in the creed. Full of divinity and power, he "comes down from heaven" and is born among us. The problem with a "descending Christology" is that it tends to overshadow Christ's real humanity. The danger is to see Jesus as basically "God in human clothing." God uses the humanity of Jesus like a cloak or instrument to work out the divine plan. Jesus's solidarity with humanity in its real struggles and sufferings can be lost and obscure the critical role of his real humanity.

In "ascending Christology," God unites to himself a real humanity in Jesus Christ. Scripture and our Catholic faith tell us Jesus is human in every way but sin. What does this mean "like us in all things"? Some guidelines for thinking about the nature of Jesus were hammered out at the Council of Nicea in AD 325. The council said Jesus has two natures: the nature of God and the nature of man. These two natures are hypostatically (inseparably) united in one divine person (the second person of the Blessed Trinity). Two natures, one divine person.

"Ascending Christology" attempts to see Jesus from below, in his humanity. If Jesus truly has a human nature, then he must have a human consciousness, he thinks as humans do. He must reason, ponder…figure things out. Jesus could not have known the world as we know it today through science. (When asked when the "end would come?" Jesus said, "I don't know. That has not been given to me.") If his consciousness is truly human, then it is finite, limited. He was tempted (Luke 4).

What I find so inspiring is Jesus smells like us. He really suffers, rejoices, grows angry, and fearful. And yet…he accomplishes the mission he knows he has been chosen to do, namely, in his death and resurrection. Surely, Jesus is absolutely exceptional in his humanity. He knew himself to be more than a prophet. He embraced his role as Savior of humanity. But he did all these things as a human being. We are saved by one like us! And so I can turn to Jesus who knows my limited human heart because he had one of them as well.

Dear Jesus. Truly you know the human heart. Give me courage when my heart grows faint. Give me faith when all seems dark. Give me love when my heart is empty. Give me hope that, in the end, "all will be well." Because you did it, Jesus! You died for us and now you live!

Let Him come to you this week.

CHAPTER 3

Being Catholic

Am I a Catholic?

Do you remember the day the world witnessed the election of Pope Francis? I remember it very well… Francis greeted the world with his first words "Buena sera." Good evening. He bowed his head and asked that we pray for him right then and there. He seemed kind and humble. The news reporters, many of them hardened journalists, distant from their Catholic upbringing, seemed almost exultant in reporting the event. One after another happily confessed to the cameras that "I myself am a Catholic, and I have never seen such joy etc." Or "I was raised Catholic, and this moment is very important to us." They were almost anxious to have you know that…*they were Catholic!*

Maybe it was the same feeling that "everyone is Irish on St. Patrick's Day." But I don't think so. Something deep was stirred that day. This is the church Christ has given us, a church that is for every race and culture and country. This church is the hope of humankind in times of darkness and trial.

So you're reading this book. What does that mean? Are you looking for God in your life? Has the Catholic faith called out to you? What is a Catholic anyway?… Here's a partial list of things that are Catholic. There's a whole lot more to mention, like joy, peace, forgiveness, etc. But here are some basics. See if you hold to these:

- Catholics are Christians.
- We believe Jesus is the Son of God, the second person of the blessed Trinity.
- Baptism begins a life of union with Him.
- Catholics believe most everything other Christians believe but sometimes more.
- Catholics believe Jesus is the head of the church, and we are the body (so there is only *one* church).
- Catholics believe Jesus wanted someone to "steer the ship" through human history, so He gave us Peter and the apostles (and their successors, the pope and the bishops).
- Catholics believe Jesus gave us seven sacraments to experience God's grace (love) when we receive them.
- Catholics follow a moral code given by Jesus and guided by the teaching of the church.
- Catholics are sinners and need God's mercy.
- Catholics go to confession when they have sinned, and Jesus forgives them right then and there.
- Catholics have to go to mass on Sunday. Keep holy the Lord's day.
- Catholics believe the bread and wine become the body and blood of Christ at mass. Jesus feeds us with Himself. (This part is really Catholic!)
- Catholics are generally no better than anyone else, and sometimes we're worse! But God holds us responsible for more.
- Catholics believe this life on earth is a preparation for union with God in the eternity of the Kingdom.

So what if I'm not there? What if I don't believe all that stuff? I was baptized, but nothing much ever came after that…am I Catholic? The answer is *yes*. The grace of baptism will never go away for you. You are forever a child of God with Christ as your light. But the question back to you is *do you want to be Catholic?* Do you want to start again the Catholic walk?

May I suggest something to you? Just come. Just walk right in and sit down. There is no test to pass, no money to pay. This church is just as much yours as anyone's. Call this place your spiritual home and *come!* Talk to a priest about your questions to determine if you'd like to be a Catholic. God will do the rest. God will come to you with His grace to show you the way. Give God a chance, okay? Listen to the music. Hear the gospel and say the prayers (ask the person next to you to help you with the book). Welcome! You're home. Watch now what God can do!

Ash Wednesday... The Big Tent (A Message to Priests)

We just celebrated what seems to me to be one of the weirdest yet most touching days of the liturgical year... Ash Wednesday. We saw a large company of baptized Christians. Many have been out in the world living their lives far from church bells and Sunday mass. But then that Wednesday comes around. For some reason, they stop everything and come to receive a dirty thumbprint on their forehead that tells everyone they are sinners.

Go figure! Of all the things that might bring them to church: a potluck supper, Eucharistic adoration, a conference on prayer. What do they show up for? Ashes! What's happening here? I think the action of receiving ashes has become the people's way of claiming their Catholic heritage. It's a powerful little package when you think about it. They're in church, they hear the gospel and homily, and they get this unique sign on their foreheads, and then maybe even Holy Communion.

As a younger priest, I must confess a secret indignation at what seemed like taking the "easy way." I started to wonder why people didn't come to mass or confession or retreat or novena, etc.? Didn't they see the truth and beauty of our Catholic way of life? There are ready answers, of course, like materialism, indifferentism, lack of faith in the divine, moral relativism, and the sinfulness of the church.

These are judgments which I believe have much truth (and here I usually add a judgement of my own...how about "carelessness"?).

There's a resentment that we priests can harbor toward those who practice their faith in this way. Haven't we wanted to confront the sullen guy at pre-Cana who makes his fiancée miserable for his having to be there? Don't you want to give parents who fail to bring their child to mass after First Holy Communion a piece of your mind? Have you experienced a seventh grader who doesn't know the Our Father? Haven't we priests made cracks at Christmas Mass poking "fun" at all the "visitors"?

The simple fact is we don't know how people got where they are. We can guess, but it's only guessing. We don't know what Mom or Dad did or didn't do for their religious faith. We don't know what angry word or stink eye some priest or parishioner gave them at just the wrong moment. What problems have they faced all alone, what decisions they made not knowing of God's grace and providence? A help for me is reflecting on what happens on that wonderful day, Ash Wednesday. It's like opening day for trout season! The stream teaming with fish, the church is filled with the people who don't usually warm to the things of religion. Why do they come? How did they know? I mean, they didn't read about it in the bulletin! Something is happening here.

Could it be that people have an inner sense that, for at least this one time, they can stand before God and know that God sees them and welcomes them just as they are? The ashes speak to them. They're proud to wear them. It's a moment with God. It's a moment that says they matter. "I have a right to those ashes because I'm a sinner...we're all sinners!" Can't you feel their embarrassed hunger to acknowledge something? And what is that? A need for God? A need to belong? A need to say something to the world?

And we have that fleeting chance to let them know how precious they are to God. Precious like the tax collector in the back that dares not raise his eyes? (Lk. 18:13). Like the prodigal son who only asks for permission to feed the pigs? (Lk 15:18). Like the children the Lord longs to gather in his arms? (Lk. 13:34). They don't need our judgment. They need to know that God knows why they are there. God sees differently than I see… God sees their hearts.

Got Hope?

What does it mean *to have hope?*

The common everyday meaning of hope has to do with a *desire* for some particular thing to happen for me or for others. For example: "I hope it snows all night so there's no school!" or "I hope the bills make the playoffs" or "I hope he calls me for dinner" or "I hope this medicine works."

This kind of hope is similar to "wishing." "I wish I could putt (sing, dance, pray…) better." In other words, it is my desire for improvement at something. Now to the degree that a certain result lies in my power to achieve, then, it would seem, if I applied myself, "I would have every hope of succeeding." But more often, we use hope to express our best wishes for ourselves and loved ones, hopes that are by no means certain. I hope you: win the lottery, do well on your SATs, get the promotion, meet up with her at the party, find those car keys. And to that hope, a friend would respond *good luck.* Good luck because "chances are" it might not happen. The New York Lottery is fond of playing on this "hope" of a win. "Play the lotto because… Hey, you never know."

This is not what Christians mean by hope. Hear the words of the *Universal Catechism*: "Hope is the virtue by which we desire the kingdom of heaven and eternal life as our happiness, placing our trust in Christ's promises…not on our own strength" (1817). Scripture says, "Hold fast the confession of hope, for he who promised is faithful" (Heb 10:23). In fact, Christian hope has nothing to do with wishing or chance. Through the merits of Christ's passion, "this hope (of eternal life) does not disappoint" (Rm 5:5). Hope is the "sure and steadfast anchor of the soul that enters where Jesus has already gone as a forerunner on our behalf" (Heb 6:19–20).

In other words, Christian hope *is a sure thing.* It's for sure because it is based on a promise by God—God who can neither deceive nor be deceived. When Jesus (the Word made flesh) says: "I am the resurrection and the life," "Whoever puts their faith in me will never suffer eternal death," "I am going to prepare a place for you and then I will come back and take you with me," *He means it. It's a sure thing.* He's not kidding around. He's the *way*, the *truth*, and the *life*.

So hope is based on the Word of God (the promises made through Jesus Christ). It is, of course, preceded by faith. *Faith* gives us the power to believe in the promises. *Hope* now desires those promises as real and attainable. And these two give rise to *charity* which, given the certainty of the promises, frees us from ourselves and our selfishness. We are then able to love God above all things and our neighbor as we love ourselves.

Mercy: More than You Deserve

So I say to you "I'll give you $50 if you wash and wax my car." And you say, "Deal." So you wash and wax my car, but contrary to our agreement, I only give you $30. "Hey, you owe me $20!" you cry. "I changed my mind," I say, "And besides, you used my bucket and soap!"

Besides never washing my car again, you'll continue to remind me that I owe you twenty bucks. Why? Because we made a deal that is recognized by law. I was legally obliged to pay you $50 for services rendered (in a larger case, you'd take me to small claims court). So knowing you'd probably tell everyone in Webster that I'd stiffed you, I finally decide to pay you the full amount. Our friendship will still need repair, but at least *justice is served*. Justice is giving to another what they deserve or have a "right" to.

We get the idea sometimes that justice is the highest form of human relationship...to give everyone what they deserve makes for a happy, well-ordered society. An eye for an eye, a tooth for a tooth. But in the Christian perspective, justice is the minimum that is expected of us. It's no big deal to be "just." We are called to a higher level of relationship. We are to be a people of mercy. *Webster's* dictionary defines mercy as "kindness in excess of what is deserved or demanded by fairness."

We see it everywhere in the Gospels. Jesus tells us: "Love your enemies, do good to those who persecute you" (Mt. 5:44). "Father forgive them, they don't know what they're doing" (Lk. 23:34). "If someone asks for your coat give them your shirt as well, to walk a mile, walk with them for two miles" (Lk. 6:27). The father put the gold ring and royal cloak on his wastrel son because "He was lost but now he is found." The laborers received a full day's wage for just one hour's work (Mt. 20:8). And St. Paul marvels at the mercy of God when he declares "that while we were still sinners and enemies of God, Christ died for us" (Rm. 5:5).

Think back. When have you received mercy? Here are some examples:

- You totaled the family car with a careless turn into a tree. Your father's first words are "Are you all right? That's all that matters."
- You were caught cheating on an exam. University rules call for your expulsion. The professor arranges for you to take a different exam under his supervision.
- Your "job performance review" was terrible. Your boss tells you not to be discouraged; he says he'll work with you. He says he thinks you've got the "right stuff."
- You went to confession and told the same sin you've committed one hundred times before. You feel like a total failure. You feel like you'll never be the person God wants you to be. The priest tells you, "God is using this weakness to grow the beautiful flower of humility deep in your heart. How beautiful you are to God!"
- Your wife tells you in tears that no matter how hard it is sometimes to live with you…she will never stop loving you.
- You've said a terrible thing about someone quite close to you. You would cut your arm off if you could just take back those words. Your friend/sibling says, "I forgive you. But please don't talk to me like that again." You burst into tears. You've just received that precious gem…mercy.

We are called to acknowledge God's mercy in our own lives (the countless times I've received more from life and God than I ever deserved). And in the joy of the resurrection, we have the grace to offer mercy to those who have offended us in some way.

Share Your Faith

So there's a lull in a conversation with friends, and someone you know, but not all that well, asks you, "Have you accepted Jesus as your Lord and Savior?" Everything stops, doesn't it? Like a sudden wind that knocks you off balance, you struggle to respond in some appropriate way, but you really are at a loss for words. Catholics especially find it hard to answer this question. "I *think* I have" might be our answer. Pressed further as to when and where you accepted Jesus, someone might say, "Well, I go to mass on Sunday," "I don't cheat anybody," "I give to the United Way," "Oh, I don't know."

I don't think it's through any lack of faith that one is left in confusion. It's just that we show our religion and faith in a different way. Taking Holy Communion at mass is probably the premiere moment for Jesus and me in the week. Yes, *there he is*, my Lord and Savior! (Chances are, our inquiring friend would not understand this answer.) And just before that, we turn to each other and say, "The peace of Christ be with you!" and we smile at each other and somehow we feel Jesus is with us. That's it. That's Jesus and me. And is He my Lord and Savior? Of course, He is!

However…that's not enough. You see, our faith is a gift that is meant to be shared. Christianity is not just about "Jesus and me"; it's about Jesus, you, and me, all of us together. Why else would Jesus leave the ninety-nine safe in the meadow to search out the lost sheep?

So how do we uptight Catholics begin to share our faith? It starts with an attitude of affection. We have to like our neighbor, to genuinely care how they are, to be happy when they are happy and sad when they are sad. Not that everyone is our best friend, but everyone can count on us to be in their corner. We want goodness to find everyone.

Once we have our neighbor fixed in our hearts as "brother" or "sister," we can speak to them as to a friend—because that's what they are (people just know it when someone approaches them in kindness). Next, we need to check our memory bank for the times God has popped up in my life. These are moments of joy or sorrow, success or failure, where I cried out to God and He heard me, or a joy beyond all expectation filled my heart. These are my life's faith stories, my God history. These things I know, not because I read about them, but because they happened to me personally. These are the things that Christ asks me to share with my neighbor when the Holy Spirit moves.

Sooooo… Some time you might consider:

- Telling a friend or coworker who's facing sickness or sadness or some worry in life, "I will say a prayer for you each day this week." And then do it!
- Telling a troubled teenager about a time in your own youth when things seemed impossible. But "You can do this. I'll pray and God will help. I know because God has helped me" (2 Cor. 1:4).
- Inviting a friend to come to mass with the promise of "breakfast on me" afterward.
- Sharing with someone what you have learned in life that relates to your faith (telling your story about: telling the truth, purity in relations, going out of your way to help, etc.).
- Let people see you make the sign of the cross, saying grace before meals, blessing your children.
- Do something for others. No expectations for a "thank you"; just a kindness that speaks all by itself.

You'll know what to do. The Holy Spirit will whisper it to you.

Why Believe?

I've been playing with the outrageous announcement the church proclaims every day but especially at this time of Easter: "Jesus Christ is risen from the dead."

The science we rely on to help us understand the physical world tells us that such an event cannot happen, given the laws of nature. Surprisingly, science has no objection to "resuscitation" (the return to bodily life of a corpse that was once thought dead. Lazarus, friend of Jesus, was resuscitated. Unfortunately, Lazarus would have to die again). Science allows for that possibility.

That is not what the church proclaims. The church boldly announces that the whole Jesus is alive, body, mind, and soul, never to die again. She declares it to be a true historical event. The resurrection is a "fact." So why should we believe what our senses can never verify? Actually, we do it all the time…do you believe your spouse when she says she loves you? Is it a "fact" when your friend says "I was there. You must not have seen me." When the state trooper stops your car to tell you the bridge is out up ahead, is it then a fact for you?

Why do we believe something is for real when we've never witnessed it? Isn't it because we know the person who's giving us the information…and we trust them? When you think about it, isn't that how we come to know most things? We trust they're telling the truth. Sunday after Sunday in the Easter season, the gospel tells a story of Jesus appearing to his disciples. Why should I believe them? I mean, he died on the cross two thousand years ago; they buried his body like any other corpse. How can I reasonably know that Jesus is truly alive and with me?

Here's what helps me believe:

- Jesus said it would happen.
- The apostles were totally surprised by the resurrection and gained nothing but persecution by spreading the news. Thousands of martyrs would follow.
- The God who is revealed by the death and resurrection of Jesus is so contrary to anything humans could ever think to cook up. ("Your God, let himself be crucified!")
- The church (for all its human failings) has never wavered in proclaiming that Jesus Christ is risen from the dead even in times of great suffering.

- The gift of faith creates a willingness in me to submit to a truth that guides my life in a hope-filled way (before that, I had nowhere to steer my ship!).
- Over time, this faith has provided the experience of a deeper love for God and neighbor that never would have happened otherwise.
- Faith in the resurrection has brought me into contact with people who have shown me a love and goodness that can only be compared to the love of Jesus Christ.

With these thoughts in mind, I take the leap of faith. And even this leap is caused by God's grace. He helps us jump!

Now, dear friends, be ready because once you say "yes" to the Easter message of eternal life with Christ, we "bind" ourselves to living according to his teachings ("religion" from the Latin, *religare*… to bind). That means: loving enemies, caring for the poor, faithful spousal love, seeking social justice, forgiveness to all who harm us, trusting God to watch over us, being there for those in need, etc.

Being just small human beings, inclined to selfishness, how will we ever live as Jesus taught? All I can say is "something happens." Over time, we get drawn out of ourselves and begin to live for God and others. And there's a happiness unlike anything the world can deliver. Please know that God loves you right now. Right where you are this moment. All he asks is that we surrender to that love. Let it conquer you, wash over you, free you.

Awhh, Mom, Do We Have To?

Remember when your parents would tell you a certain thing had to be done, and it had to be done right now? "And this afternoon, we are all going to Grandma's house to visit." And the response from this pouty fourteen-year-old boy was usually… "Ahh, Mom, do we have to?"

Maturity and the spirit of generosity had not yet taken full root. Everything that didn't meet my personal agenda was a huge distraction and inconvenience. Only the authority of a parent (especially a stern father) could curb the self-interest that underlined most of my choices. Do I have to?…was the spirit I brought to so many things. Surprisingly, that didn't faze Mom and Dad too much. They didn't care how happy I felt about going to Grandma—just that I went. I guess it was because in their own way, they knew that good things would come from it, things that would inform this teenager why it was "a good thing to do."

Things like your grandmother grabbing your cheeks and looking deep in your face, saying, "Tim, I'm so glad you came to see me. You know I get awfully lonely by myself some times. You made my day. I love you so much." "Thanks, Grandma. I love you too." *Do I have to* becomes *I want to*. What causes this change of heart? I think it is the realization that I have the power to make a real contribution to someone's happiness or well-being. My efforts, here and now, can make life better for others. I want to be about that kind of living. That is the beginning of stewardship and hospitality. What is hospitality? It is the habit of seeing in my neighbor an honored colleague, a valued teammate in the not-so-easy task of bringing goodness where there is strife.

Sounds lofty and complex? It's really simple stuff, like smiling at the mother whose child is fussing in church, like moving into the center of the pew so the person needing to sit doesn't have to crawl over you, like saying your name and asking someone theirs, like hearing a call for help and responding because you've gone from "do I have to?" to "I want to."

So what about mass on Sunday? A child would ask… "Do we have to go?" And the church (our mother in the faith) says… "If you need to ask, the answer is yes, you have to go." "Why?" the child asks. "Because the Lord said so," the church responds. The third commandment says it—"Remember to keep holy the Lord's day." Jesus said, "Do this in memory of me." Like any good parent, God only asks these things because they are good for us.

My hope for us is that by now we see the wonder and privilege to worship the Lord on Sunday. Why do we go to mass on Sundays? An adult answer might be: "Because…"

- I want to show God that I love Him.
- I need to thank God for the goodness I have received this week.
- my life is hard, and I need God to help me. We talk about this (God and me) at mass.
- oftentimes I get something I didn't know I needed.
- I believe in the Eucharist. This is the body and blood of Jesus Christ. God becomes my food.
- I need the people gathered with me on Sunday to experience more fully what it means to be members of the body of Christ.
- It sets my whole week in the right direction.
- I get lost without mass on Sunday.
- I'm all alone without this experience once a week.
- Sunday is the day Jesus rose from the dead. Now I have hope of eternal life. I just have to pause and think about this on Sunday.

Going to mass is only the beginning of "keeping holy the Lord's day." Sometimes we need to look at how we live our Sundays of the week. Do we make them special days of peace, family, rest, and recreation? A real spiritual renewal and reorientation toward God can happen on such a Sunday.

Why not try this? Set aside next Sunday—all day. Plan only those things that will bring rest and relaxation and participation in the Sunday mass.

CHAPTER 4

Habits and Virtues

What is Theology?

Last week, we celebrated the solemnity of the Most Holy Trinity. This week, we will visit a most important doctrine of the faith, the Most Holy Body and Blood of Christ (Corpus Christi Sunday). So it might be well to look at what goes into these essential teachings and how they developed. (These teachings have a history that gradually took shape over several centuries.)

It may surprise you to hear that the titles of "triune God" and "the Body and Blood of Christ" were not spoken in this catechetical manner for the first few centuries of the church. St. Peter, if asked to give a definition of the Most Holy Trinity, might have answered, "the what?" The celebration of the body and blood (the mass), was earlier referred to as "the breaking of the bread." We must be careful here. The reality of both of these teachings was present from the beginning. But the titles and their precise explanations developed over the early centuries. The church was in search of a vocabulary to accurately talk about what she already "knew in her heart."

This searching for the right words (which correctly state what faith believes) is called theology. You might ask, what comes first, faith or theology? The answer is they come together. St. Paul describes the partnership of faith and theology (words). Speaking of our ability to believe in Christ, he says, "But how can they believe in him (Christ) if they have not heard? And how can they hear without someone to preach?… Thus faith comes from what is heard, and what is heard comes through the word of Christ" (Romans 10:14–18).

But the purpose of words is to carry the meaning of what already *is*. So words come second to what is believed but only by a heartbeat! For how else could we understand our faith without words to express it? Remember in sixth grade when our teacher made us prove we understood a new word? She would insist "now put that word into a sentence!" *Then* she knew we understood.

But how can we be sure our sentences about faith are correct? There is a little drill that keeps us on course.

1. What did Jesus say? The words of Christ and the New Testament (and the Old Testament as well) contain the Word of God. It is on this word that faith begins. We believe on the authority of these words spoken by God in sacred scripture. Theology calls this the "canon" forming the first basis of "revelation."

2. The words of Sacred Scripture can be turned in many directions. Some interpretations are very insightful and full of great spiritual benefit. This is the job of theology, to think and pray over what God intends to "reveal" there. And then it articulates in words ever-deeper understanding.

3. But what happens if some theology gets it wrong? Or what if two theologies contradict each other? Great theological disputes have taken place about the simplest of bible quotations. (For example, Jesus's words to Peter, "You are Peter and on this rock I will build my church" [Mt. 16:18] has caused great debate amongst theologians.)

There is a safety net. Revealed in sacred scripture (and recognized by theologians!) is the promise to the church that the Holy Spirit will "lead you to all truth" (Jn. 16:13). Tradition (the second part of "revelation") has placed in the apostles and their successors (the bishops) a divine gift to teach without error the matters of faith and morality. Theology calls it the "magisterium." It is comprised of the pope in union with the bishops throughout the world. It is also called the "teaching church." Thus, the whole body of Christ, the Church, can be assured of the true faith in Jesus Christ.

Sorry for the lecture!

Faith Leads to Worship

Let's take another look at what worship and adoration is about. It's important to understand what we're doing and why. The Catholic Catechism explains, "To adore God is to acknowledge him as God, as the Creator and Savior, the Lord and Master of everything that exists, as infinite and merciful Love…to adore God is to acknowledge in absolute submission the 'nothingness of the creature' who would not exist but for God."

In short, God is our all, our everything. But how do we love and serve a God we cannot see or touch? God has to help us. He has to give us something to hold on to as belonging to Him or at least pointing to Him. And He has. "What can be known about God is plain to see, for God Himself made it plain. Ever since God created the world, his invisible qualities, both his eternal power and his divine nature, have been clearly seen; they are perceived in the things that God has made" (Romans 1:20).

So worship begins by acknowledging that all we see, all that is, comes from God. This is called "natural religion," and it is as old as the human race. And so humans have made offerings to the "gods" of the mountains, the sun, the moon, the fields, the oceans… But God wished to elevate his beloved creature man and woman to a new level of knowledge and love of God. And so God did the unimaginable. He became a human being named Jesus, "the image of the invisible God" (Col. 1:15).

1 John 1:2 tells us, "The Word of Life was made visible; we have seen it and testify to it, and proclaim to you what was with the Father was made visible to us." And so our worship of God becomes personal now. It focuses on the person of God who is Jesus, God become human flesh. Yes, we worship God when we worship Christ because… "through him (Jesus), God created everything in heaven

and earth, all things were created through him and for him. He is before all things and in him all things hold together" (Col. 1:17). Jesus sort of summarized all this when, in answer to the Apostle Philip's request to show him "the Father," Jesus said, "Philip, when you see me you see the Father" (Jn. 14:8).

But *how* do we worship God. What do we do? In ancient times, we would collect the finest fruit of the harvest and burn it, turning it to smoke which rises to God. Or we would slay a bull or ox or goat and place it on the altar of sacrifice. Basically, we would give God the best of what we have. And here is where God absolutely astonishes us with his love. God puts in our hands the very offering he wishes us to give him...his only Son, Jesus.

You see, Jesus is God's gift to us and our gift back to God. His life was lived in total dedication to the will of the Father. Jesus was the Lamb that was slain. His death on the cross, freely accepted as the way his Father, was to reconcile the human race to his burning love, forever becomes our offering of worship to God the Father. Where does this happen? The mass. God gives us his Son. We give him back to the Father. And Jesus wants this to happen until he comes in glory. "Do this in memory of me."

Are You a Good Seed?

I keep thinking of that little seed in the Gospel. "Unless the seed falls to the ground...and dies. It remains just a grain of wheat." Jesus is telling us the purpose of the seed (its meaning) lies in "what it becomes" (John 12:21). We see this happening all around us this summer. The kernel of corn becomes a corn stalk, which will bring ears of corn. An acorn begins the long journey of becoming an oak tree. The grain of wheat, the apple, pumpkin, tomato, wildflower seeds...all of them must die if we are to have the wonderful gift they bring. (Seeds in a bag? What good is that? Spread 'em around and be amazed!)

Jesus tells us in this short brilliant image that we humans must "die to ourselves" and begin "living for others," and it's when we do this that we discover who God made us to be. It brings a peace the world does not understand, a happiness no one can take away. And…it makes the world shine a bit brighter. I can't overemphasize how critical this "dying to ourselves" is to discovering who we are and finding the path ahead for our lives. It starts early in life when our parents teach us to "share," "to shake hands and make up," "to be gentle." Later on, when life deals harder things, we're challenged to "forgive," "to go the extra mile," "to comfort others," "to persevere."

With practice, this thinking first of others becomes a habit, a character strength. It comes more easily with time, and a quiet peace happens in one's conscience… I've done the right thing. I feel clean. On the other hand, sadness comes most often when we realize we've put all our eggs in the wrong basket. The one marked "more for me."

It's a cliché I know, but have you ever met someone with great financial resources, comforts, and possessions, the envy of all, yet someone who never learned the lesson of the seed? (It's all there in the story of the rich young man (Luke 18:18–29). So in the meantime, go be a good seed this week.

- Stay a bit longer with "that person" who tries your patience.
- Think ahead as to what might please your spouse. Do it.
- Smile when you're not feeling happy.
- Say a prayer for someone who hurt you.
- Find a way to encourage a young person to use their gifts.
- Give some money away.
- Someone disappoints you for the hundredth time. Smile and find a kind word for them.
- Sit with someone who needs company.
- Think of a generous reason why someone might be so annoying. Forgive them.
- Presume you've been that annoying too. Ask for pardon where appropriate.
- Go out of your way to be kind to people who wait on you. A smile and a kind word can really help someone.
- Know that any impulse to kindness and generosity is a grace given to you by God.

As If God Were Appealing Through Us

These are the remarkable words St. Paul speaks in the first letter to the Corinthians. He calls us "ambassadors for Christ." Picture yourself sitting in that large circle of chairs at the United Nations. To your left is the ambassador from Russia, and on your right are the ambassadors from Nigeria and Poland. You are there as ambassador for the Kingdom of God. Really. Your words, your deeds are meant to introduce these people to your country. You represent a nation that experiences the love of God living and active amongst its citizens because of their faith in Jesus Christ. The people of this nation are not perfect but try to love one another because they have first been loved by Christ.

St. Paul does not call us preachers, we are ambassadors, living, breathing citizens of a nation that God has invited all humankind to claim as their home. And that's what ambassadors do…they represent in their very selves the country they come from. We don't spout slogans; we *are* our message. So what's the point? The point is: *you* are the instrument God uses to help people know Him. Think about how you experienced God's love in your life. Wasn't it through *people*? Your parents, friends, teachers, priest. Weren't they ambassadors for Christ to you? Christ appealing to you through them? Parents, I don't think you see yourself having so important a role. Jesus expects you to introduce Him to your children, your siblings, and coworkers.

Wait a minute. I'm no saint! How can I give Christ to others? Just be your best self. Be the person who cares what happens. Be the person who looks out for others. Be a sign of hope when everyone else is quitting. Be the one who finds the light rather than cursing the darkness. Be the person who's not afraid or embarrassed to admit their Catholic faith means something to them.

So how about this?… Sometime this summer, at a picnic or a reunion, tell a story about what happened to you when came to mass one Sunday. It could be funny or meaningful or anything in between The point is it's *your* story. (God will remind you what story to tell.) Then…say something like… "Ron, if you're looking for a church where you can give your cares to God, come and see how it feels." Or simply, "Sunday mass has made a nice difference for the week that follows."

Remember, you were appointed ambassador; you didn't run for election. So let's do our job. Ask away. You're doing this for Christ the Good Shepherd, and we are his sheepdogs…uh, I mean ambassadors!

Bad Moods—What to Do?

I'm sitting here on a Monday looking out my office window. It's currently eighteen degrees outside under gray skies. I'm searching for something to talk to you about that you might find of some interest. I'm not finding it.

Things feel kind of flat this morning. The Sunday masses, rite of Christian initiation of adults (RCIA) class, and two baptisms are all done. COVID concerns are popping up everywhere, it seems. The cold and gray will be here for what? Three or four more months? I'm starting to get into a mood. Ever happen to you?

So let's talk about "moods." *Webster's* dictionary is always a good starting place: "Mood: a temporary state of mind. A pervading quality of feeling at a particular moment." They come in all shades, don't they? Good ones, happy ones, sad, bored, excited. But the ones we talk about the most are the bad ones. (Just like the news we watch on TV; good news doesn't get the headlines.) We expect to feel good/okay in the normal course of things and pay it no attention. It's the bad moods we're most aware of.

I think it depends on how old you are to see how bad moods can affect us. Remember when as a child, you were sick to your stomach? Christmas failed to bring a new bike? A rained-out baseball game? We felt the world was about to end. Teenagers collapse at the sign of a pimple, a "C" in English class, being laughed at in the cafeteria, getting snubbed by the "in group." Later on in life, disappointments with work, a failed relationship, one's "status" compared to others can send us off, not just to a mood, but to a permanent way of viewing life as a disappointment.

Combine that with the way we are wired (some have a natural tendency to see life's cup as half empty), and soon we discover there needs to be a governor that regulates and disciplines our moods. Otherwise, they carry us off. Our feelings begin to tell us who we are. With age, we begin to discover that's not true. We've been up and down and all around enough to realize "this too shall pass." Think back. Aren't you glad you didn't act on your first impulse? You didn't quit whatever; you didn't make that angry phone call; you waited till the mood passed. And it did pass. Didn't it?

So here are some tips on how to deal with bad moods.

- Don't believe the message that we should be happy all the time. The entertainment industry makes millions portraying life as it should be—endlessly exciting and fulfilling. It can be at times, but not how it is reflected on TV.
- Don't think there's something wrong with you if your moods happen to be sad. Hey, life has these moments. We can learn from them but not be ruled by them.
- If the moods last and become a constant worry or sadness, *talk to someone about them.* Sometimes just speaking our feelings to a friend can be like a medicine. It connects us to a trusted person. (That person may be a priest or doctor if you think it might help.)
- Remember, moods pass. Like the clouds overhead, they roll on—it's just temporary "weather."
- Please, please…don't make any life-changing decisions in the spell of a bad mood. Wait (an old priest friend of mine went a step further to say, "Don't ever make an important decision after the sun goes down. Wait until the next morning." Why? Because our enemy "fear" moves better at night).
- Lastly. You are a child of God. You are loved. That fact remains. Moods don't.

Guess what? I'm outta that bad mood!

Good Enough

A friend of mine said his company, which prides itself on its exacting standards, was losing clients to inferior competition because their products were cheaper and "good enough." It started me thinking about when we can settle for good enough…and when we can't. As I think about it, "good enough" is okay in many situations. Bottle openers, pencils, socks, hammers, cigarette lighters, ballpoint pens all provide a function that does not require any special brilliance. One is as good as another.

However, some things by their nature require the very best. Things like…heart surgeons, airline pilots, psychologists, and how about…lion tamers? There's no room for "good enough" here. Can you see the surgeon standing over your mother or father saying, "That's good enough—close him up"? I'd look for another doctor.

Or how about husband, wife, father, mother…what's a good-enough mother? And Christian, what's good enough there? It seems many times, we settle for good enough when we say "I'm not very religious, but I'm spiritual." Or "One religion is as good as another." Catholicism? It's a "good enough" religion. How that squares with Jesus's words, "Unless you eat my flesh and drink my blood you will not have my life in you," is a mystery to me. Or, "Yeah, I go to mass. Not all the time but every couple of weeks is…(you guessed it)… good enough."

It all boils down to love. It doesn't ask what's enough. St. Paul tells us love has no limit to its patience, its generosity, its hope, its power to endure (1 Cor. 13). Love wants things just right. Consider a bride coming down the aisle to meet her husband, her hair, her dress is perfect—for him. Your baby's crib and blankets need to be just right, not good enough. This is what love does. It gives everything. Can you imagine Jesus, love incarnate, saying, "Okay, I'll take the agony in the garden, the scourging at the pillar, and the crown of thorns. Forget that death on a cross thing. That will be good enough."?

So we say we love God. What's good enough here? Every day is an opportunity for a new beginning. May I suggest that we have a great opportunity to grow in our faith and love of God.

Goodness In, Goodness Out

Certainly you've heard the adage "you are what you eat." And our computer geeks are fond of saying "garbage in, garbage out." The point being in both of these sayings…something becomes the sum of what was put into it. Good health comes from a good diet. A dependable computer program requires good data input. (The Bible was on to this when three thousand years ago, it said, "You reap what you sow.") It works like that with our spiritual life too. We are greatly shaped by what we think and hear, see and touch. What we allow to enter through our senses creates the raw data for the kind of person we become.

So for example:

- Child psychologists tell us that hours spent watching violent images on television elevates the likeliness of children acting out violently.
- Constant attention to a handheld computer game or iPod inhibits a young person's ability to interact with real people.
- Nonstop images of negative, argumentative relationships create the impression that this is how people naturally interact. Yelling, whining, cursing, name-calling becomes the norm. Talk radio is full of this stuff.
- Pretty much any television called "reality TV" has little grasp of what's really real.
- Yet, love of music, theater, intelligent discussion, *Downton Abbey* (!), great sport creates openness to a healthy psyche.

So why not put a stop to the "garbage in, garbage out" syndrome? Why not dedicate ourselves to "goodness in, goodness out"? What does this mean? It means putting a guard over what we let our eyes see and ears hear. I'm being literal here. Change the channel or turn off the TV when it becomes crass or trashy. Walk away from conversations that are only meant to hurt others reputations. Put away the electronic games or instruments when people are present to talk to.

Guarding what you let in through the senses creates an interior sense of order and goodness. St. Paul points to the governing of the senses by the Holy Spirit. It brings about the fruits of "peace, patience, kindness, generosity, purity…" Compare that to how you feel after watching a fighting cage match on TV? Spending four hours on some PlayStation war game? Going from one porn site to another on your computer? Reading what gossip is out there on the Internet about your friends and enemies?

Let's be honest here. There's a dark pleasure in these things. (Why else would millions of people go there?) But deep down, we know this is not who we are. We're all junked up. It feels dark and smarmy. There's a simple remedy. Go somewhere else. Some place that puts good stuff in. You decide. But some examples could include good music, entertainment, books, fishing, friends, travel, nature, winemaking, conversation, prayer. Look around, God made a whole bunch of stuff to capture our interest.

Are there any dark places that feed your senses in a way that hurts your soul? I bet you've tried to avoid them but fallen back. Try again. Keep trying. Ask God to help you find another way. God will answer that prayer.

Hospitality: To Be Appreciated

In one of my first parishes, I was part of a team of catechists that led the Rite of Christian Initiation of Adults (RCIA) classes for people exploring the possibility of becoming Catholic. It was there I learned a rather humbling lesson in hospitality. You see, each catechist was responsible for their particular class—the room setup, handouts, any audio/video needs—each teacher did their own thing, if you will.

I remember when it was my turn to teach, I took quite seriously the proper preparation of classroom content. As for the room we would spend the next ninety minutes in, I felt it was adequately prepared if the heat was on and the lights worked.

In contrast to this were the lessons taught by Sr. Anne Marie, our pastoral associate. Not only were her classes impeccably prepared, but the room in which we would meet would always have something beautiful greeting us when we arrived. One week perhaps, a burning candle safely placed in a nest of autumn leaves, another time perhaps, a picture of some natural beauty or some person of nobility or dignity would greet us. And always there would be some small token of food and drink over which we would pause to eat and converse. You just felt good to be there. You felt appreciated.

I always thought, *Gee, Sister, this is really nice, but you didn't have to go to all the trouble.* She would only smile at me and keep up these special efforts. I am embarrassed to say that only now do I get it. Sr. Anne Marie was practicing the virtue of hospitality. And the power of this virtue does not lie in the donut holes or coffee being served; rather, it was in the care poured out upon those who would join her that day. She was showing us by example how to honor people. How to create an environment that brings comfort and peace… Why?… because you are a child of God and her brother or sister in Christ. And believe me, you really felt it in her presence.

This is hospitality—treating one another as another Christ. And the wonderful thing about this virtue is that most often and most effective are the small things done out of love. Things like these during Sunday mass:

* Smiling at the person in your pew as you take your seat. Giving a warm "hello" as we greet those around us at the beginning of mass (they are there for the same reason you are…to try to find God in their life).
* Sing. Yes, you. Sing. Do you recite the *Happy Birthday* song at birthday parties? Of course not, you sing them. Should we give less than that to God and our neighbor? Do you see that not singing is in a way holding yourself back from joining the celebration?
* Learning someone's name—even if you've failed ten times before. What better way to honor someone than to know their name?
* Just showing up. You may not know this, but people miss you when you aren't there. Really! I've been asked many

times by parishioners, have you seen so-and-so? "I haven't seen them in a few weeks. I hope they are well."
* Being patient and understanding of a mother or father trying to calm a fussy child.

You are a good person. You know what to do.

"If You Had Been Here..."

I can't imagine that Martha was anything but heartbroken and angry with Jesus when he showed up four days late to save her brother Lazarus. She and her sister Mary had sent an urgent message for him to come, "Lord, your dear friend is sick."

The two sisters were particularly close to Jesus. (Remember the dinner? Martha fumed away in the kitchen while Mary sat talking with Jesus.) They were themselves...no pious holy card figures. "Why weren't you here, Jesus? Our brother would never have died!"

And what was the reason Jesus gave for his delay? "For your (the disciples) sake I am glad I was not with him so that you will believe" (That Christ has power over sin and death) (Jn, 11:15). What follows, of course, totally amazed everybody; Lazarus comes back to life. So what's the point for you and me? Well, unless you are like Jesus and can raise dead people back to life, you'd better be there. What's the line from the movie *Annie Hall*? Eighty percent of life is just showing up. Not being there to win everyone's attention, not to do anything special, *just be there.*

We don't believe that about ourselves, do we? That we make a difference. Many times we think, *Who am I that people would want me to be there? What will I say? What should I do? They won't care if I'm not there.* But it's not that way for people who love you. Your presence is a comfort to them. I remember my father's face buried amongst hundreds of people in the stands as we faced our archrivals in basketball. It was such a comfort to know he was there...as we lost the game.

You see, you don't need to say anything. You don't need to be witty or profound or anything. Just be you and show up. Love will do the rest.

Show up for the following:

- Dinner with the family
- Dance recitals/games/birthdays
- Bedtime/prayer time for the children
- Parish picnics/movie nights/walks with a friend
- Work/work/work/
- Mass/mass/mass!

Why show up? Because we're less when you aren't there. And you don't know how many people are missing you.

"I'm Spiritual but Not Religious."

Have you heard someone say that to you? It seems to be a common phrase these days. Many feel it best expresses their view of life. Let's take a minute to see what they mean by that. Let's try to see the good thing they are pointing to because they feel it's a thoughtful, virtuous way to live life. And it is.

"I'm spiritual." It means a person is aware that there is "something" in this world beyond what we can see and touch. There is something that can't be spotted by our microscopes or telescopes or chemical analysis. It's a spirit that has a meaning and beauty that makes human life worth living. It seems very active in those "peak" moments of life…falling in love, the birth of a child, etc. One gets the sense of being connected to something bigger than them, something kind and beautiful.

The phrase "I'm spiritual" is a nontechnical term trying to describe a feeling or an intuition. When I am aware of it, I experience myself fitting into a universal, a spiritual plan. The plan is good and benevolent, and I feel happy that I could connect with it. That's not bad, eh? Really. It sensitizes people to the beauty around us. It's like a melody playing in the background. When we feel this "good spirit," we say, "I don't go to church. My church is a walk in the world around me." I think we've all found the beauty of nature touching us and leading us to the Creator. We're all "spiritual" in this sense. So what's the problem with this? It doesn't hurt anybody. There have been no wars fought over being "spiritual." My only thought at this point is there's no one to thank. It's a painting without a painter; a symphony without a composer. We're still *alone*. Ultimately, what good is that?

What happens when life turns ugly? What happens when I don't feel my spiritual side? When sorrow or sickness or tragedy strikes? When my walk in the woods is scary and lonely? When life and its demands feel overwhelming? Being "spiritual" somehow doesn't get to the depth of the human experience.

Okay, so what about "religion," and how is it different from that "spiritual" feeling? (What follows are words from someone who "believes in God.")

The Christian religion says that God has actually revealed himself to us in the history of the human race. There was a five-thousand-year-old process of recording God's actions in human history called the Bible (the creation of the heavens and earth, calling a people to a special relationship with him (the Jews), and finally coming to live among us in human form [Jesus Christ]). In this process, we are given a pretty specific description of who God is and how God acts. Time and again, Jesus would say, "The Kingdom of Heaven is like…" and there would follow a picture of some aspect of God, right down to his name—"Father." One of his stories describes heaven to a king who has a banquet, and we humans are invited guests.

Christians can't walk away from this Revealed Word. We are tied to this belief about God and human existence. The word "religion" itself has the notion of being "tied to" something (*religare*—Latin, meaning "to bind together"). "Being tied to" what has been revealed is really important because it gives us the knowledge to know who God is. The people who hold this knowledge and act according to its instructions have what we call "religion."

But aren't there many religions? Yes, there are many religions. So then, it doesn't matter which one I practice, right? It does if you want to know the whole truth. They all might have something of the truth, but they can't all be right (the resurrection of the dead for Christians is totally different from the reincarnation for Buddhists).

It is here I think we go back to two things. True religion, unlike "being spiritual," has to deal with the following: (1) The staggering beauty of human life in both its joys and sorrows—what best explains who we are? What is love? How can there be suffering and yet still a God we can honestly worship? (2) How does one come to the knowledge and love of such a being?

Answers to these questions are beyond our ability to fathom. God has to help us. He has to give us something that will touch the deepest recesses of the human heart and open us to His mystery. It's called the gift of faith and it was delivered to us in actual words by another human being, Jesus Christ. "This is my beloved Son. Listen to Him" (Luke 9:35).

In Vitro: Up Close and Personal (Another Message to Priests)

I found myself waiting for a small class of high school juniors to gather for a lesson on "mindfulness" and how it can lead to prayer. As students filed in, one young lady took her seat, settled her backpack, and fired off a question, "Father, would you please tell me the Church's teaching on in vitro fertilization?" (IVF) Being somewhat savvy to "diversion tactics" (get the teacher off topic so nothing gets covered that day), I took her question lightly and gave her a minimal response. "It's complicated," I said, wanting to get on with class. Her tone and expression intensified, and I began to realize this was something she wanted to seriously discuss (we'll call her Sarah). So I proceeded to speak to the class about this rather difficult issue. Unprepared for this lesson, my seminary studies and what little I'd read over the years were my talking points. You all know them:

- It is God who creates human beings. The immortal soul comes as His gift, not the result of a lab technique.
- One does not have a "right" to the gift of a child.

- God's way of creating human life is to partner with us humans. The man and woman come together in an act of love, and God's plan within nature then takes place.
- Conception is the complete beginning of a human being. The in vitro process often leads to unwanted, discarded human life, direct or indirect abortions.
- This is a slippery slope that can lead to social engineering, a human race reflecting current social prejudices (gender preference, racial discrimination, etc.).
- The Church urges medicine to find ways to "facilitate" conception without replacing God, nature, and the spouses.

As you can imagine, Sarah's eyes were glazing over by my third point. "So I guess the answer is…the Church says no. Right?" "Yes, Sarah, but you need to know that every child born of in vitro fertilization is loved and wanted by God and their parents. They are God's children." "Well, that's good to know," Sarah smiled, "because I'm an in vitro child. And see that boy in the back row? That's my twin brother." She spoke warmly of her parents who went to such lengths to bring her into the world.

Well, now… I stood silent, trying to process the moment. I'd known in vitro from a moral theology book. Suddenly, I'm meeting in vitro up close and personal—Sarah and her twin brother, Matt. And that wasn't all. She opened up her laptop and clicked around to show me a picture of Sarah smiling and holding identical twins on her lap. "These are my twin brothers in Indiana." (Her mother had donated fertilized eggs to a couple in Indianapolis.)

So what's the point of the story? The issue of IVF is complicated. Looking at these happy young creatures, Sarah and her brother Matt, I could only imagine the joy those children must bring to their parents. I wanted to rejoice with them all. "For she who was barren has also conceived" (Lk. 1:36).

Yet, I don't doubt for a moment the Church's moral assessment of IVF. She is right in placing human conception in God's hands. I see the slippery slope of scientific manipulation; how it can make the human race into someone's misguided vision of a "perfect society."

Abortions will happen even when not intended. And yes, the Church must continue her education about this complicated moral issue. But…the fact remains, a growing number of our brothers and sisters are here thanks to in vitro fertilization. Sarah was eager to share her origins and family happiness (millennials are so open!). I wonder in the end if it's even any of my business to know such things.

I guess the point is to acknowledge that Sarah and Matt are here, and they want to know about Jesus Christ. They want to know they have a place in a loving Church. How we priests get to know and respond to these children will help determine whether they do, in fact, come to know Him. But one thing is certain, every child is wanted and loved by God.

Judge Not, Lest You Be Judged

There is a teaching in Catholic moral theology, rooted in the Bible, that tells us we have an obligation to let our neighbor know when they are committing sin. It's called fraternal correction, and the obligation occurs first with those who we know to be Christian and hold the same principles of behavior as we do. Scripture says in effect we are doing them a favor. The hope is they recognize their failure and return to right behavior. By this, you have saved your brother/sister. To remain silent is an offense against them.

Now some of us respond to this injunction more vigorously than others. They like to correct people. The problem is sometimes we do the "correcting" behind their back in conversation with others. Jesus addressed this when he advised us to take the log out of our own eye first, then we would see clearly to help remove our neighbor's splinter. Others of us (perhaps most) are inclined to "just go along." We close our eyes to the bad stuff happening around us. We don't want to "get involved," "it's none of my business." This is what happens to me, and I bet to you too.

So how do we do the right thing here? How do I know when to speak out and when to remain silent? Certainly, the gravity of the situation would require us to act. Serious danger to innocent persons, great scandal to children, a major injustice or unfairness, observed cruelty to others…all require us to step forward to witness to goodness, to protect innocence. I think most of us see our duty here. With God's help, let us be up to the test.

But there is something else happening here. You see, along the way of "correcting" someone, we can often end up "judging" them. It is at that point we've gone too far, for judgment belongs to God. It can be hard to distinguish between the two (judging/correcting). Let's see if we can find some guidelines.

- To tell my coworker that he has his facts wrong or his statement is inaccurate is correcting.
- To say "you're lying" or "you're a liar" is judging.
- To encourage someone to not give up or to "keep on trying" is a way to correct. To call them a lazy quitter is to judge.

It would seem if there is a label attached to the behavior one is concerned about, chances are I'm judging another person. So why can't we judge people? Because we just don't know the reasons why people do the things they do or sometimes the desperate situations in which they must choose. And lacking that knowledge, the goodness or evil of their actions is known only to God. (Remember the woman caught in adultery? "Has no one condemned you?" said Jesus. "Nor do I. Go and avoid this in the future." This was correction, not judgment.)

One key that helps a bit is to try as St. Paul says to "bear with one another," to accept people as they are with certain weaknesses and faults. Not that we close our eyes to wrongdoing but that we "love the sinner." It's love that brings someone to their senses, not judgment.

It's Okay to Fail, Just Try Again

We're all familiar with the good intentions that go into New Year's resolutions. Also familiar is our failure to keep them for very long! Many of us experience the same thing with our attempts to "sacrifice" for Lent. Perhaps that's what's happened to you this Lent. Your good attempts to "give something to God" haven't worked out. Discouragement follows, and we go away a little sad.

Perhaps a new perspective about Lent can help. You see, God doesn't need our sacrifices. Rather, God wants our happiness. God wants us to be free. This freedom is, at its root, an "indifference" toward ourselves and the unnecessary attachments that preoccupy our time and energy. Free of these, our hearts have time and energy to welcome God's grace.

What is grace? Simply put, it is God's love acting in our lives. It reminds us of who we are (His child); it opens our eyes to see His presence in the world. God's grace moves us to "get beyond ourselves and our wants," to see others as gifts to be loved and cherished.

So the key to the season of Lent is to ask for the grace to let go of what may keep us locked on ourselves. We've all developed habits in life that keep ourselves comfortable and self-contained (*my* time, *my* space, *my* schedule, etc.). This Lent, is there one thing (not two or three) that we might surrender to God in love that would make us "available" to be lifted out of ourselves? This surrender frees us up to be there for others. *My* time, once so precious *to me*, becomes a gift we can give to our children, our spouse to God (prayer). Jesus nailed this when he said, "Whoever loses their life for my sake, will find it" (Mt. 10:39).

Even this little "giving up" will hurt a bit at first. The bond of selfishness and habit is strong! This, too, requires God's grace. To fail and to start again. In fact, maybe this Lent, God wants you to experience your failing…and rising. Do not become discouraged. God loves even your failed attempts!

Now the good news is it can eventually become a joyful discipline. We rediscover some wonderful things we had forgotten, things like: a clean conscience, a clearer sense of purpose to our work and why we do it, a softening of our hearts toward those we find easy to judge (knowing now our own weaknesses), a better understanding of how to use the things of this world properly, without excess or hoarding.

So what is this joyful thing that happens? As I mentioned above…freedom! Freedom from always having to satisfy your own wants and a clear space to feel what God intended you to be. How wonderful you are when you get out of your own way!

So let's start again (and again!). Say goodbye to one small thing that you know needs to go (at least for a while). Make a conscious offering of it to God in prayer. (For example, "Lord, help me to smile more even when I don't feel it." Or "Lord, I'm really good at finding fault. Help me to see the good and be thankful." Or "Lord, this money was going to get me some new shoes. I don't need them. Someone else does." Or "Lord, I want to really love you more. Here's my time spent watching TV, show me how to pray.")

"But, Lord, I'm gonna need your grace."

Are There Spirits Out There?

This will be a different article and not one I'm crazy about writing. It's about "the spirit world" and what we as Catholics believe about it.

Over my years as a priest, I've had several people approach me (young and old) about an experience they've had with a spirit. They heard a voice or saw a shadow or silhouette in the room. Some have played with an Ouija board and gotten "a message." Some have gone to seances to connect with the spirit of someone now dead. What are we to believe about such things, and how are we to treat them?

First off, the Bible and our faith tell us that yes, there are intelligent spirits in the universe. They go by various names: angels, powers, principalities, demons. Both the Old and New Testaments testify to the existence of these "created" spirits in a realm beyond our human way of existing. A familiar example would be the Angel Gabriel, who served in the classic capacity of an angel… "God's messenger" to Mary. We believe in the guardian angels given to each of us to watch over and protect (Mt. 4:11, Mt. 18:10). We also hear of course of "evil spirits" who, Catholic doctrine teaches, are created spirits who failed the test of freedom to serve God prior to the fall of Adam and Eve.

Okay…so the question for many is "Can I get in touch with the spirit world?" Various reasons are given why someone would want this: (1) I want to know if my deceased loved one is at peace. (2) I'd like someone to tell me if I should make a change in my life or not. What is my future? (3) It's fun in a spooky kind of way to entertain at a party. Our faith teaches us to be careful here. There is a danger for some well-intentioned person to turn to the spirit world as a source of power separate from God. A person begins to rely on incantations, seances, horoscopes, tea leaves, and crystal balls to show them the future or answer life's questions.

So what's wrong with that? Simply put, it goes against our trust in God's providence. God loves us and seeks a personal relationship with us as our Father. Turning to an Ouija board to show us our future is telling God "he's not enough" or "trust in God but consult your tarot cards, just to be sure." There are some things we aren't supposed to know. God has chosen to keep some things hidden from us. For example—when God will call each of us home. There is wisdom in this. Knowing some things would keep us from living our everyday lives. "Not knowing" helps us turn to God in faith and trust.

Psalm 131 tells us, "I have not gone after things too great for me. Like a weaned child on its mothers breast so my soul lies within me." So trust in God. Be content in knowing what you know. Pray for those things about which you are concerned, and know that God who "knit you in your mother's womb" (Ps. 139), "knows what you need even before you ask" (Mt. 6:8).

Lastly. Are there spirits? Yes. Do they mess with us sometimes? Very seldom. (I think a rectory I lived in some time ago had a very timid spirit living in the attic. Really I do. He stayed in the attic and didn't bother me at all.) You need to know, however, that any spirit owes its existence from God. God is not rivaled or challenged by spirits. God has complete charge of the freedom He gives to all his creatures and sets limits for them according to His good will.

In the end, there is only one spirit to which our knees must bend, the Holy Spirit.

Light a Candle or Curse the Darkness?

There is a prayer league called the Christopher's, who have as their motto "It's better to light one candle than to curse the darkness." What a wonderful motto. I bet you can explain its meaning without much coaching…spread the light, not the dark. But what does that mean in practical ways? It means there is a choice to be made in many of our human activities, a choice between goodness and meanness, or truth or lies, or generosity and selfishness. Sometimes the differences are muted, but they are there.

There are of course "neutral choices" or choices of preference (the soup you eat or the toothpaste you buy) that don't spread light or darkness. But think for a minute how many times in the day we are confronted with opportunities for goodness or evil in the twinkling of an eye.

- Do I say something positive about a person or join in the litany of faults that others enjoy telling?
- Do I watch something funny or human or beautiful on TV or search out programming with ultraviolence, fear, or lewdness?
- Do I try to find something hopeful in a difficult situation or enjoy describing how terrible things are?
- Do I wait for the smallest opportunity to "be offended," or do I take any personal slights as coming from someone whose day is probably harder than mine? Someone who needs my patience.
- Do I take the old comfortable path of minimal effort, or do I try to make something beautiful or excellent?
- Do I give a person the benefit of the doubt, or do I presume their motives are small and mean?
- Do I enjoy getting angry and being hurt, or do I try (not always successfully!) to ignore or forgive?
- Do I grab that parking spot or let someone else have it?
- Do I enjoy a whining ("It's just not fair!"), or do I try to point to what's wrong in a way that people are invited

to correct ("Why don't we try this? Let's try to make this better")?

Did you know that the light is more powerful than the dark? (Sometimes we wonder, don't we?) Think about it though, what is darkness but the absence of light. Darkness is removed by lighting a light. Try that at home. Wait till dark. Make sure all the lights are out in the room. Then light a single candle. The entire room catches the light however dimly. See it flicker on the wall! Darkness has no power over light…so long as it shines.

"Dear God, help me to learn to love your light. Help me to learn that I carry your light. Oh God, use me to spread your light."

Light a light or curse the darkness. You choose.

Lonely? Of Course

"It is not good for man to be alone." These remarkable words are spoken by God in the book of Genesis as he seeks for a way to brighten things for a sad and lonely Adam. So God created Eve, and she and Adam became "partners."

Problem solved? For a while. But then it happened. Our first parents chose to walk away from God who created them. And that's when the sadness and loneliness of life settled in. They can no longer look at each other. They take up wearing leaves to hide their nakedness. Loneliness is born. Oh dear. There's a tear in our hearts. We want to connect with others, but who is there we can trust to know us completely? (Haven't many of us at some time assumed we'd found "Mr. or Ms. Wonderful"?) Finally, we meet someone who is endlessly fascinating and fun and who delights in our every thought. How soon we discover they (and we) are not as perfect as we thought.

Do you begin to see the peaceful coexistence of the world's peoples hangs on the common conviction that we are created and saved by God who calls us His children? Without the assurance of the love of God upholding creation and calling humanity to Himself, we're left with a profound mistrust of one another. Not even friend, lover, husband, or wife will put to rest our craving for love and completion in this broken world. God created the human creature whose ultimate purpose is to know and love our Creator. He is our *all*.

So what do we do? Here's where people can get lost. Some people will medicate their loneliness (food, alcohol, pills, etc.). Some will try to fill it with people and constant activity. Some go shopping! Why not travel? Why not accept your loneliness? It's part of life. It goes along with all the other moments humans experience. "There is a season and a time for every purpose. A time to be born, a time to die, a time to laugh, a time to weep." A time to be lonely. In fact, loneliness can add an unexpected blessing in our lives. It can force us to know ourselves, to truly embrace who we are (the good and the bad, the happy and sad). We stop running away from ourselves. Being alone is not so bad. (Maybe you've learned a little of this in these days of COVID isolation.) Best of all, loneliness can invite me to reach out to God in prayer. To confide in God what you'd speak to no other…knowing that he hears and understands all of you.

Do you know who the loneliest guy in the world is? It has to be Jesus. Who on earth could possibly understand who he was? Who could ever know the weight his mission placed on his shoulders? What must have been his loneliness in the garden that terrible night? Who could ever comfort Jesus? But he was never alone, for he knew his Father. (How often the scripture refers to Jesus spending the night alone in prayer to his Father "who sees in secret.")

Lonely? Of course. Embrace it. Make friends with it ("Sister Loneliness," St. Francis might say). You'll be surprised how it will make you a better person; it can make you aware of the loneliness of others. It's called compassion.

Last thought. There's no loneliness in heaven. God will permeate every speck of our being. "For now we see as through a glass darkly, but then face to face: now I know in part, but then I shall know even as I am known" (1 Cor. 13:12).

God sees you…and loves you always.

Love Your Enemies

Nowhere, ever, will you find the "love your enemy" in the law for any nation, any organization, any religion…only Christianity has this command. These words were spoken by Our Lord Himself, not to living saints, but to his disciples, rough fishermen, common people. He speaks to you and me.

Think for a moment…do you have any enemies? I mean real enemies, someone who wants bad things to happen to you. Someone who tries to hurt you? If you lived in Israel, or Palestine, you could answer "yes." For the Jew, it would be "the Palestinians"; for the Palestinian, it would be "the Jews." For the Serbians, it's the Croats (and vice versa). And on it goes, Huttus vs. Tutsis, Christians vs. Moslems, and here in America, we could say at times even Democrats and Republicans.

How about you? Do you have any enemies? I'm hard-pressed to answer "yes" to that. I have people who don't like me or don't trust me (and me toward them); perhaps they are a rival, but I can't say I know anyone who is my enemy. Does this clear us from the Lord's command? "I'm ok here, Lord, I don't have any enemies." I don't think so. In the same way, Jesus expanded the other commandments of the Torah—from thou shall not kill to shall not grow angry, from thou shall not commit adultery to thou shall not even look lustfully—so now my "enemy" becomes someone who doesn't necessarily "hate" me but rather someone who "stands in my way." My enemy becomes someone who thinks differently than me. Someone who makes me afraid, someone who, yes, doesn't like me. Someone who hurt me, and by golly, I'm not going to forget that.

And what do we do with this new "expanded" version of enemy? We avoid that person. We gather people around us who feel the same way about that person. You can see how this natural response to an opposing force begins to divide the human family. Fear, retaliation, mistrust become the atmosphere between families, coworkers, political parties, cultures, religions, and nations. How can this situation, given human nature, ever change? Or perhaps do we even want it to change? (Isn't it easier to keep my enemies my enemy?)

No. Jesus says, "Love your enemy." But how? (Please know I'm trying to do these myself, and many of you are much better at this than I am.) Thoughts to help me love my enemy:

- To love doesn't mean to feel "sweet" toward my enemy. Bottom line is that it means to want what is good for them, "that they be well."
- Who knows what hurtful events have marked their lives. Perhaps their response to me is really just them trying not to be hurt again.
- Inside every human being is someone who (because we are made in God's image) wants to love and be loved. Every one of us. So my "enemy" is like me!
- How would I wish to be treated by this person? Do that for them.
- In the end, God is bigger than my feelings and fears. If He commands it, then He will help me do it.
- It's going to hurt. It is part of the cross we carry for love of Christ.
- No one wants to have or be…an enemy.

God help us all with these things. In the end, Jesus wants us to love like Him and His Father.

Positive Thinking: Faith's Gift

As I've mentioned to you, my father was an insurance salesman who overcame many personal qualities (he was very shy and prone to pessimism) to become an outgoing, confident, highly knowledgeable insurance agent. Along the way, he found a couple of motivational books that helped him get beyond his personality weaknesses: N. V. Peale's *How to Win Friends and Influence People,* and *The Power of Positive Thinking*. These were life-changers for Dad, and he insisted his pouty teenage son read them both.

I hated them. They seemed so '50s, so "establishment" as my generation would caustically remark. "Just think positively, and everything will turn out peachy keen," I mocked. "Tell that to the guys in Vietnam," I said with righteous fever. Get real, Dad.

That was a long time ago. As in many things, I've come to see my Dad was right. You become what you believe in. You acquire the qualities of what you take into yourself. For example, if I spend my time watching dark, violent, or lustful images, I begin to have a hunger for these things in real life (ever see one of those cage matches on ultimate fighting? We become excited by human blood and pain. Horrible).

If I pride myself in finding something wrong in any given situation, I begin to prefer the negative. I feel validated by it, proclaiming myself a "realist." Our spirits are shaped by what we take in to our minds. On the other hand, if we feed on things that speak of goodness or generosity, forgiveness, mercy, sacrifice, joy, and light, our spirits will have that same beauty.

Regard the face of the social worker who has devoted her life to helping the poor, or the face of the old nun who has taught thousands of schoolchildren, or the face of the symphony conductor finishing Beethoven's Pastoral Symphony… They are beautiful! Look at the face of the mother kissing her newborn…so full of love.

Now this is not a psychological trick like some chameleon becoming the color it touches. It's real. The light is real. Goodness is real. Love is real. And…guess what? (This is the Easter part!) This light has overcome the darkness. Love wins! How do we know this? Because Jesus Christ is risen from the dead. "The Light has shown in the darkness, and the darkness has not overcome it" (Jn. 1:5).

So what do we do now (and all year)? We take in the light, not the darkness—you know the difference, you can feel it. We give forth the light, we walk with those in darkness and negativity helping them to see life's goodness.

And all this "positive thinking" is not just some childish wishful thinking. It's the rock on which we live our lives—Jesus Christ is risen from the dead.

Let's get to work.

Out of Alignment

Pictures, as the saying goes, are worth a thousand words. Whether it's about "a feeling" or "an idea" or "something we believe in," it helps to get a picture in our mind that captures the essence of what we're thinking about.

So I was thinking the other day of what the faith teaches about "the effects of original sin." You remember original sin, right? In the mythic story, Adam and Eve disobeyed God's command to refrain from eating the fruit of that tree. It's the God-inspired picture of an event; no one was there to record. It is a great mystery.

The Catechism tells us that one of the effects of original sin has been the wounding of our human nature. That means the creature, man, made in God's image, has forfeited his original holiness and justice and "is wounded in the natural powers proper to it" (reason and will) (Catholic Catechesis #405). In short, we suffer ignorance about who we are, and in this ignorance, we are inclined to sin. This leaning toward sin is called "concupiscence."

So here's my picture. See if this makes any sense... I had an old VW "bug" way back in college. Great little vehicle—started up every time. One problem, it was out of alignment. Driving down the road, if you let go of the wheel, before long it would pull left and take you into the oncoming lane. It wouldn't happen all at once, but you could feel a leaning. Like the car had a mind of its own, it pulled you into the other lane. To counteract this, you had to drive with the wheel pegged to the right. This would keep the car in the proper lane heading straight.

It is the same with us humans. If we let go of the wheel, if we don't take control over the direction of our lives, we eventually "pull into the wrong lane." Each of us experience this pull in our own way (the classic "pulls" are called the capital sins—pride, envy, anger, gluttony, lust, jealousy, and sloth). What's yours?

The church's teaching about the effects of original sin makes great sense. It's a pull, an inclination. Going our own way, without God's will to guide us, sooner or later we fall. Everyone sins. Don't be shocked that you have this tendency to sin—everybody has it (except Jesus and Mary—but that's another story!). We're in a battle. Be ready to fight. Some battles we win; some we lose. But we don't give up the fight.

The good news is that we've got the power to overcome this misalignment. Be aware of the pull "and keep our hands on the wheel!" Pray and recognize your tendency and ask God to help correct your alignment. Ask for the strength to avoid the places and things that approach you with the familiar enticements that sin brings with it. Don't be discouraged if it takes a while to keep in the proper lane. A priest might be able to help you here. Certainly, the sacrament of penance/reconciliation (confession) is a great source of strength and realignment.

Lastly, do really fun things. The devil hates it when people can laugh at themselves and share friendship with others who are keeping their hands on the wheel.

This Is Not a Dress Rehearsal

Maybe it was because my father held a rather strict hand in raising his children. Maybe it was the preaching old Fr. MacIntyre would deliver Sunday after Sunday in my parish growing up. Maybe it was just "the times" back in the 50s and early 60s. Whatever the reason, I've always been a little afraid of the words in the creed which says God "will come again in glory to judge the living and the dead." It tells me that what I do in my life will be examined by God who made me. It's called "judgment day" when "every one of us will have to give an account of himself/herself before God" (Romans 14:12).

I don't think we give enough attention to this warning. We in the United States, we can easily forget that this life of ours will come to an end and then God will have a few questions for us (I don't have the slightest idea *how* this will happen…but faith tells us, somehow there will be a reckoning). Other generations had this urgency in their bones. My father, who saw life and death during the war, was fond of telling us that "life is real and earnest. This is not a dress rehearsal. This is it."

So many today live a passive response to this urgency. "Whatever," we say carelessly. Or "That's a long way off. I can't be bothered thinking about the end." Or "My life is mine to live. Back off." We have a choice as to how to imagine our lives. In the end, I think it comes down to two basic options (see if this image makes any sense…it will take you back to your post-high school days). Think of a college or certification class that will help you develop a certain knowledge or skill. And you have a choice…you can take the course for credit, or you can simply audit it.

Auditing has a certain appeal, doesn't it? It's cheaper, there's no essay required and, best of all, no test. All you have to do is sit there. Take whatever you want and leave the rest (I audited a course one summer. It was great! I can't remember a single thing it taught, but I met this really cool girl). *Or*—you can take it for credit. This will cost you more in time, money, and sweat. And…you will have to show what you've learned to get the credit.

So why take the credit course? Because it leads somewhere. It takes you to a new place. You now have something you own, and with this achievement, you can advance a career, secure a future, and realize what you are capable of.

So the question is: are you in this life for credit, or are you merely auditing? Jesus has a story that might help you decide. Read Matthew 25:14–30 (really, I mean it; it'll take three minutes). An owner gives three people a different sum of money to conduct their portion of the business of running a vineyard. The first two take the money and use it in a way that increases the value of the vineyard. The third fellow takes the money and buries it, thinking if he just gives it back, that will be enough. Well, guess what? It wasn't enough. He fired him. The master wanted a return on his investment. He wanted to see some sort of effort to advance the cause of the business.

Jesus tells this story to wake us up. God has given you a life to live. He's blessed you with certain talents and gifts. What have you done with it?

It's never too late to begin. All God asks is that we try. He'll take care of the rest. This is it. No dress rehearsal.

Your Conscience

One of the most critical tasks of a parent in raising a child is to ensure a proper understanding of what makes us most human—our conscience (take a moment right now. How would you explain to a child what their conscience is?) Maybe this article can help.

The Catechism of the Catholic Church has a mini-class about conscience and its proper formation (Article 6. Moral Conscience). There you read, "Conscience is a judgement of the reason whereby the human person recognizes…what he knows to be just and right… when he listens to his conscience, the prudent person can hear God speaking" (#1777).

In short, our conscience comes from the way we think about things. It doesn't really kick in when we observe the sensate world ("What time is it?" is not a matter of conscience). But something changes when we consider the presence of good and evil. Math and science can't reach these matters. We have to use a different measuring stick—our sense of right and wrong.

Here's where things can get confusing if you don't have a strong conscience. You see our mind can be a tricky thing. It is prey to many impulses that influence what it thinks is "right reason" or thinking correctly. The passions (God-given feelings that accompany certain actions): hunger, love, anger, jealousy, pleasure, etc. can affect our reasoning. (How many times did "having one for the road" seem like a great idea?) The problem is, we don't think right. So where does right thinking come from? Where do principles of justice, truthfulness, fair play, kindness come from? They come from a source beyond ourselves—the source of meaning and being itself…they come from God.

There is a beautiful description of the voice of conscience as it comes to the human intellect. *Gaudium et Spes* (Joy and Hope), written at the Second Vatican Council, states, "Deep within his conscience man discovers a law which he has not laid upon himself but which he must obey. Its voice ever calling him to love and to do what is good and to avoid evil sounds in his heart at the right moment… for man has in his heart a law inscribed by God…his conscience is man's most secret core and his sanctuary. There he is alone with God whose voice echoes in his depths." Conscience carries the voice of God.

But can't there be different ways of seeing things? How can we be sure it's God's voice and not our own leanings and passions talking to us? Like your child, consciences must be properly formed. It takes a lifetime. A big part of conscience formation comes in knowing the sources of moral guidance: the ten commandments, Jesus's teaching, natural order, traditional wisdom, seeking reliable information, and finally, prayer. But above all, conscience is formed by knowing and believing that we were created to be with God, and the goal and happiness of our life depend on doing God's will. Trusting then that the Lord will echo His will in your heart, be in peace.

So, parents, sit with your children. Tell them about their conscience. Let them know they can feel it in the happiness that comes when they do the right thing. Also, they must listen to the voice of their conscience when they feel the heaviness when they've done wrong. It is the loving correction of Our Lord. A clean conscience is our steady rock in the midst of life's storms.

Curiosity Killed the Cat

One of the common human habits we all share to some degree is curiosity. At first glance, it can seem a harmless practice; in fact, good things can come from it. For example, a student is curious about what causes thunderstorms or hail. It moves them to pursue a deeper knowledge of weather. Your doctor is curious about your blood pressure and why it's so high. This is good curiosity.

Bad curiosity (or what we call nosiness) is something else. It's a habit of inquiring about people—concerning matters that are none of your business. "I wonder what he makes at his job?" "Where do they stay when they go on vacation?" "Who is she dating?" "Why are those two friends?" "I wonder what their marriage is really like."

Why do we do that? Because it brings us pleasure. Such knowledge about others brings a certain power; now we know something that unlocks a side of them they choose not to reveal to us. On the surface, it can seem a harmless habit, "I just want to know more about this person" (so why not just ask them?).

But let's be honest. Many times, this inquisitiveness is a desire to find some "dirt." Much of the grocery tabloids and the Internet rely on our hunger for steamy details about celebrities. Paparazzi make their living delivering photos to feed our curiosity. There's a certain pleasure in seeing someone weak or out of control (the German's call it *shadenfreuda*—pleasure derived from other's problems).

Why can curiosity be sinful? Because it violates two virtues we owe to others. The first is justice. People have a right to privacy about personal matters. Prying eyes and ears serve to "steal" something that doesn't belong to them. Thou shalt not steal. Secondly, charity. Scripture tells us we are to do to others what we would want done to ourselves. How do we like when someone wants to know our thoughts and feelings about matters we deem to be private? It's not theirs to have. So that same respect must be shown to others.

But there is another matter sinful curiosity can cause. Sadness. Think about it. "Love does not rejoice over wrongdoing but rejoices with the truth" (1 Cor. 13:6). There's a certain darkness that happens when we wander into people's lives in search of private things. We become less a good friend to that person (or at least a less respectful fellow citizen).

When we hear and judge others on matters obtained through curiosity, it can affect the way we interact with that person. We become less transparent because we "know something." Over time, cynicism and suspicion can grow about anyone and "what they're *really* like."

So what can we do to curb our curiosity appetite? These might help.

- Recognize what you're doing. Ask yourself why you want to know or am I just curious?
- Would I like someone else to be inquisitive about me as I am about them?
- When prying thoughts about others occur, change them to quick prayer for the person.

- Note: parents have a right to be curious about their children. You are their guardians. (Teens need a little more slack!)
- Avoid conversations that deal in private matters about others not present. Gossip.
- Be glad you don't know stuff! It frees you up.

To Listen Is a Gift

God gave us the sense of hearing. We share with the animal world a sense that alerts us to the world around us. We hear thunder, and we know rain will soon fall. Sirens tell us of some emergency situation. Music soothes our soul or stirs emotion. A whisper gives us someone's secret thought. To live without hearing is like eating a sugar-free cookie; we lose the gusto and subtle meanings of life.

But we take it for granted, don't we? These days, we are overloaded with sound. Our brains have to choose whether to merely "hear something" or to really "listen." Remember musak? It was that bland orchestra music that played on elevators to keep everyone calm waiting for their floor. Did you ever give it a listen? Of course not. No one ever said, "Oh, they're playing my favorite song!" It's only when we *listen* that we receive creation around us. To hear a bird's song is different than listening to it. That bird…is singing…its song! How lovely.

Our brains make that same choice with people, whether to merely hear them, or to really listen to them. We've all developed skills that give the impression we're listening. We nod at the right times; we comment as appropriate. But many times, we're simply waiting for our chance to start talking. Or hearing one or two sentences we think we already know what someone is going to say. And rather than listen, we're preparing our response to them while they're still talking.

That's why to truly listen is a gift to the one who is speaking. Have you had the experience of being listened to? What did it do for you? I bet it touched you, gave you the feeling that you had connected with someone. Being listened to (especially with a friend) can lighten our burden—finally! Someone else knows what I've been carrying. Now you both carry it.

By the way…that's one of the healing powers of telling your sins to Christ in confession. Yes, God gets in here too.

Sometimes, when we really listen, we hear something from the Holy Spirit. Something God wants us to hear. I've had that experience. A friend came to me at a very busy moment as I prepared for an important interview. "Tim, listen to me," he said. "I have to tell you something. They're going to push your buttons. Stay calm and don't be a wise guy." I listened, and it was just what I needed at that moment. The Holy Spirit used my friend.

So husbands/wives, listen, really listen, to each other. You don't have to fix things right then. Your full attention to what she's saying is a gift. You might even reflect her feelings with words like "that must have really surprised/shocked/bothered/helped/made you happy."

To be listened to is wonderful. Try it with your children. Withhold judgement for those moments…just listen. They'll know you are with them in whatever they are going through. Scripture tells us, "Bear one another's burdens" (Galatians 6:2). As you develop your listening skills, it will improve your prayer as well. You will look back over your day to see those moments when you heard something God wanted you to hear. If you were listening.

CHAPTER 5

Parents and Children

Your Family: Bigger than You Think

Jesus, Mary, and Joseph. The Holy Family, what a team! Mary, the mother, was conceived without sin (Immaculate Conception), Joseph (a just and faith-filled man), and Jesus, God in human flesh… it sounds like a household of superheroes. They're certainly not like *my* family.

Before we look at this saintly group, let's look back a bit at the whole idea of "family." That familiar picture we have: the house with the picket fence, the kids playing in the front yard, Mom in her apron getting dinner ready, and Dad just back from work, calling out, "Honey, I'm home!" was, until recently, a common view of a middle-class home.

To go back a thousand years or so, "family" was more like a "clan" or a tribe. That African saying "It takes a village to raise a child" is evident in much of history. In primitive times, with dangers lurking in nature (lions!) and neighboring peoples (those Hatfields!), an extended family was the best way to ensure safety and a cooperative way of getting things done. We see evidence of this in Jesus's childhood. When he was twelve, his whole "extended family" in Nazareth traveled by caravan to Jerusalem. Jesus was gone from Mary and Joseph for a day or so with no apparent concern from his parents. "As they were returning, the boy Jesus remained behind in Jerusalem, but his parents did not know it, thinking he was in the caravan (with the rest of the relatives)" (Luke 2:43, 44). They returned to Jerusalem, and "after three days (!) they found him in the temple."

So what does "family" look like today? It comes in many shapes and sizes. Blended families, single-parent families, extended, adopted, etc. What does your family look like? Mine has shrunk somewhat. Mom and Dad are gone over ten years, so we are now only three (Patty, Tim, and Maureen). This is what I mean when I say "I'm visiting family."

How about your family? Big? Small? Just you? We look at photos of Christmas past, and we smile…or tear up a bit. Over the years, family changes, doesn't it? But something about belonging to a family never changes; it's where we learn how to give and receive love. St. Pope John Paul called the family the "school of love." It's where we learn to live for others and accept other's kindness in turn. Family is where we help each other come to know the goodness of God. It's been called the "domestic church."

Now here's the exciting part…real family, described above, can happen anywhere, with any group of people. Jesus himself pointed to this. Remember the story of Jesus preaching in a crowded house? "Someone told him, 'Your mother and brothers are standing outside wishing to speak with you.'" Jesus said in reply, "Who are my mother and brothers?" And stretching out his hand he said, "Here is my (family). Whoever does the will of my Heavenly Father is mother, brother and sister to me" (Mt. 12:48, 49).

It's a new kind of family. One that is intended and sustained by the will of God. The family of Christ. The Church in the widest sense, people of good will seeking to love God and neighbor as Jesus has instructed us. And guess what? This family is thicker than blood or ethnicity. It's Father is our Heavenly Father; Mary is its mother. We all are God's Children. Please help Holy Trinity Church be a part of Christ's family by the way we treat all who join us.

Grandparents. A Second Wind

My old college friends are by now well launched into their grandparent stage. I never thought the day would come when my golfing buddies would throw me off for a day at the zoo with their grandchild—and do it happily! I have to admit that feelings of "grandparenting" have crept into this old priest's heart as well.

What is it that happens to us as we approach and live out our seventies and eighties? I think we finally realize the proper proportion things should have in our life. Things that were huge when we were younger are now not so big. I mean really, how important is the Disneyland vacation now? That promotion? The tattoo? The six-pack abs? Perfect hair? The first-place finish? That college acceptance? The right car/home/kitchen? They're not nearly so important as we seniors look ahead to our final years. Those things get smaller. What gets bigger? People get bigger. And not just friends and family; humanity, wherever it exists, becomes the most important thing in the world. We belong to each other. Can't you feel it?

Then there's this deep hunger, so hard to explain. A hunger that wants to see humanity at peace. A sickened feeling when we see a child ill fed or in tattered clothes. A deep connection to the mother or father who holds a crying child. The grief of parents and siblings weeping over the tragic loss of a young person. It all touches us now because we finally realize…they are a part of us. The human family. There's this feeling like, "Dear God, we are better than this. How did we get *here*?" And perhaps most important, "What can I do to make this better?" Perhaps for the first time in our life, we see how serious it is for us to think of others. Maybe we see how wasteful and selfish has been our use of time and the earth's limited resources.

A new wind starts to blow at this stage of life. There is a felt need "to give back." Our parents and grandparents were children of the Great Depression and two world wars. They devoted themselves to making life easier for their children than it was for them. "To have what we couldn't." They succeeded.

Times have changed since then. These days, many parents/grandparents are unable to help lift their children to greater economic security. The new wind that blows isn't about economic prosperity. It's about hope. We know something about life that the young ones don't…(as St. Catherine of Siena said)… "All will be well." How can we say such a thing? "All will be well." It's a fair question. In a world so troubled on so many fronts, how can one have hope for the future? What comes next will only make sense if you believe in God (or something good much bigger than yourself).

It's this… "God so loved the world that he gave his only Son, so that everyone who believes in him might have eternal life" (Jn. 3:16). God's love "bears all things, believes all things, hopes all things, endures all things. Love never fails…" (1 Cor. 13ff). **And**… "All things work together for the good for those who love God" (Rm. 8:28). And "Jesus Christ is risen from the dead."

What do these words of sacred scripture tell us but that God started this world out of love, we messed it up, Christ came to "bear all things" and conquer sin and death. And now *all things* will, eventually, work toward the total victory of God's plan of love. Do you believe that? If you do, then you believe that for all the seemingly impossible problems of war, poverty, racism, violence against women, Zika, terrorism, etc., etc…that God would never allow the ultimate destruction of the human experiment.

Now this hope is what we need to give to our children. All will be well.

Hey, Dad

Today is your day. We're not too keen on these things, are we? Somehow it goes against what we see as our role as the "watch-over person." We've all seen holy cards of the holy family. There they are, Mary and the baby, front and center. Joseph is usually off to the side watching or standing over his wife and the child as protector. We like the background role. In fact, we can sometimes "hide" in the back when things get sticky or uncomfortable. When tears or disappointment come to the children, it's time for Mom! She's the expert in handling emotions or significant events…birthdays, in-laws, holidays, vacation plans, etc.

So what *do* you do, Dad? Can I tell you what I've seen you do? First off, you love your wife. She has the key to your heart. She is the one person who pulled you out of yourself when you were this whiney, selfish twentysomething to thirtysomething. She helped you discover that "to love" meant to "lay your life down." You didn't know that until you met her. Now your job is to make her life a joy.

The second thing is the children she gave you to hold. What profound stirrings you felt when each of your children looked up at you. Somewhere came that particular "father feeling" that said, "No one will ever hurt this child so long as I am here. You are safe with me, dear one,...do you hear that world?"

What else do you do, Dad? You create a "place" that is warm, safe, and fun. Yes, it's a place to live, but it's more than that. Your strength and love and watchfulness brings about a place in which your wife and children can blossom and grow. They don't have to worry "are we okay here?" They're free from fear because you are there. You are like the house beams, always there, quiet, holding things in place. The world is dependable...because you are dependable. You beat back the chaos.

Last on my list of things to thank you for is the fact that you didn't give into me when you knew I was headed in the wrong direction. I could bully Mom into going along with some silly scheme I thought was really cool. She would say, "Well, honey, if it will make you happy." But you wouldn't budge. "Rethink that," you would say. "That's not what we taught you." You had several other sayings that went right to the heart of the matter. Things like...don't give up... you disappoint me (ouch!)...do it the right way, not the easy way... I'm proud of you...don't worry, I'll be there...and (yes, Dad, you actually said this)... "I'm not your friend, I'm your father." Dad, you saved us from our worst impulses.

Lastly, you show us something of God the Father. You are strong, present, watching, protecting; you are our rock. You gave us a "place" of safety to discover who we are; you were strong enough to listen when Mom knew us better. You gave up your crazy ways to be our dad. We are really glad you did.

Kids These Days

There is a program on cable television called *Dirty Jobs*. It portrays a typical day at some of the dirtiest jobs in the country. The nastier elements of garbage disposal, food preparation, sanitation work, cleaning and refurbishing are there to be seen in all their ickiness.

As tough as these can be, they can't compare with what I think is the hardest job of all…raising children to be healthy, happy, self-disciplined, and kind. Yes, it, too, is a messy job, but not for the dirt and grime of the workplace. It's messy because we try and fail…and try again. It's messy because sometimes parents just don't know the best way to handle things. It's messy because we can't be certain of the outcome until some twenty-five or thirty years have shown what this child has grown to be.

We hear of the heartbroken father in the gospel; his daughter is sick unto death, "Someone please help us! Jesus, come and help my daughter." A parents' worst nightmare—their endangered child. Some of you have experienced this very event, the death of a child. A more profound heartbreak—there is none. And then…if by some chance, you do everything right and the kid grows straight and true…they find someone to love and leave you. And you wouldn't have it any other way, but it hurts.

So why would anyone want this messy job of parenting? Because it makes you into the best person you can be. Children and spouse are one of the few forces in life stronger than our selfishness. It is in raising children that you give your all. (Doesn't it take everything?) You lay down your life for them. And as Jesus says, "No greater love hath someone that they lay down their life" for those God gives them (Jn 15:13).

Monks have their chapel and their fields. Nuns have their convent and their work. Priests have their parish and their bishop. Parents have their children. Each situation works by God's plan to help us forget ourselves and live for others.

Thank you, Mother and Father, for loving us more than you loved yourself.

Parents: Don't Be Embarrassed

The fear of embarrassment causes more people to shut down and hide than nearly any other experience. To feel totally exposed to strangers, or those closest to us, for that matter; there's nothing quite like it. Think of those times when fear of embarrassment took hold of you. How about singing at mass, dancing while sober, holding hands, taking your driver's test, speaking a foreign language, getting your tax filing audited, asking someone out for the first time, that first kiss…and the greatest fear of all? Public speaking. There's a ton of them.

And what is it that grips us so tightly; that freezes us up? I think it's the possibility of being laughed at, ridiculed, or rejected. In that scary moment, we're just "out there," unguarded, vulnerable. The slightest smirk or roll of the eyes means total rejection. We've all experienced it, and we never want it to happen again. It's why children stop acting like children. Their free, silly exuberance has met disapproval. "There must be something wrong with me" is the message we get. And so we begin to protect ourselves (a necessary adjustment to life at times). But it can come at a cost of never investing ourselves in what we truly believe. We can turn our back on the things most important to us.

Why did Peter deny the Lord three times (one of them to a little servant girl!)? (Luke 22:54–62). He was scared and embarrassed. We all know the feeling.

Parents and grandparents are expected to get over this fear… if only for the sake of children and spouse. You are supposed to be bigger than your fears (or at least be willing to confront them) for the sake of what you love and hold true. But still, the feelings of embarrassment harass us. As a priest, I see it when it comes to speaking about your faith in God. Many have gotten away from the religion of their youth (when talking about loving God came as easily as speaking of your love for the family dog).

We remember the times in life we have strayed. Perhaps the practice of the Catholic faith has become spotty at best. Consequently, we feel like hypocrites when we talk about God or the commandments or prayer. "If the guys at work heard me saying these things to my child, they'd howl with laughter." So we console ourselves with the thought that at least I'm not being a phony…and we say nothing. This won't do. We need to be bigger than our embarrassment. There are some things "you just know in your bones." Stay true to them. Things like: God has given me this child. I've experienced a love for them I never knew I was capable of. When I surrender to God's plan for me (my here and now), I see how I can add goodness without embarrassment. I can witness to the God I *know from my own experience.*

Six simple things you can do with your child to witness the faith God has given to you.

1. Send your child off to school, to bed, to sports, with the sign of the cross traced lightly on their forehead. "God bless you and protect you" is all you need to say.
2. Tell your child, "I'm praying for you." You don't know what this knowledge will do for your child.
3. Ask for your child's prayers. Something like "I need your help. Would you pray that my meeting goes well today?" Kids want to help.
4. Tell your child when you've experienced God in your life. "I looked at you when you were born, and I just knew God had blessed me."
5. Share your embarrassment with your child. Something like … "You know, I'm not the best at this, but maybe *together* we can learn about God."
6. Bring your child to mass. There is no substitute for this.

Love will help you get over your embarrassment.

The Family Meal

I've said many times that creating a family and raising children is the toughest job in the world. Parents are heroes. One of the things that makes family life such a challenge is the culture we live in. Its values and goals so often conflict with the life experiences we want our children to have. Most parents want the "best" for their family. But what is the best? Current social norms encourage families to "go for it all." Sports, social media, cell phones, video games, Internet browsing, cable TV are all part of the fabric of young family life.

Each in themselves can be harmless and, at best, recreational and restorative. But as in all things, "too much" causes overload and the breakdown of the peaceful flow of human relationships. It was recently reported that teens were spending more time on the computer and cell phones than in daily sleep! A local college chaplain told me the biggest challenge he had in helping his young students was to get them to put down their cell phones and iPods to talk to each other!

In all this, we are losing something precious…the fun and satisfaction of talking and relating with each other. Strong measures to correct this are needed and will, at times, take courage and wisdom to deal with the resistance.

One step you can take is the family meal (especially on Sunday). Does your family have dinner together? Maybe not every night, given people's crazy schedules—but more times than not during the week, families should sit at a table to eat and share stories about the day or upcoming events. It's not that anyone's hilarious story or deeply meaningful comment will happen; that's not the point. What's happening is the wider event—we're caring for each other. We're learning about our lives together. The dinner table is where we show each other "I've got your back," "we are a family."

Think back. I bet you could tell five really good stories about your dinner table growing up. Funny stories, stories of tears and meltdowns, stories of deep sharing. Parents, it's up to you to show your children how important dinner together is. You're there to create memories.

One pastor I served under (a difficult man at times) insisted that I be at table for dinner at the rectory. I bristled at first, wanting to watch the evening news and eat on my own schedule. These meals over time let me see the really good man my pastor was.

- Here's an old dinner table story from my youth. We had a dog named Penny, a copper-colored dachshund dog.

This dog had free run of the backyard, and as dogs do, Penny would leave her "droppings" everywhere. As we headed out to play, Mom would remind us, "Watch where you stepped." Well, guess who didn't? No sooner had we finished grace before the evening meal that the odor told everyone someone had "stepped in it." "Check your shoes," Dad would say. Yes, it was me. No shouting or finger-pointing…just go clean off your shoes or, even better, take them off. Returning to the table, the offense having been removed, we all could enjoy our dinner.

This is the perfect image of purgatory (you can't sit at the banquet of heaven with "you know what" on your shoes). Clean 'em off, and you're welcome at the table.

The Right to Have Life

I continue to be amazed at the simple fact that you and I exist. There are some simple moments of awareness that, when you pause over them, bring out the wonder of our being here.

A young mother was having a dish of ice cream as her nine-month-old sat quietly next to her. "Watch this," she said. Putting her little finger into the ice cream, she put it to Sarah's mouth. The baby took Mom's creamy finger, and her face became a picture of unbridled joy. "Sarah loves the taste of vanilla!" Mom said. I swear the angels in heaven were jealous at that moment.

That was over twenty years ago. By now, I'm sure Sarah is not quite so gaga over her ice cream; like the rest of us, she's grown, no longer a child. We change, but we're still the same person who thrilled at vanilla.

Science tells us the human body generates a total renewal of cells every ten years…yet, we are still who we are…we are still that unique person who was born into the world. Such a mystery we are! We hunger to know, "Who am I? Why am I here? Why am I the way that I am?" No understanding of ourselves seems to go deep enough to touch these wonderings. To our parents, we are "son/daughter."

Siblings call us "brother/sister." I am "priest" to you and our bishop. You are "husband/wife" perhaps. But ultimately, there is one relationship that finally defines all of us—we are a child of God. God created us to be a person like God. We owe our total existence to Him.

Now happily, God uses people to bring us into the world. People who knew nothing of me till I was born. Mom told me I kept everybody waiting. "You were a week late," she said. "We thought you were a girl." All this my mother had to tell me, for how would I know by myself? That I would exist and be held and changed and tossed up in the air by my dad and not remember it one bit tells me that life is something that *happened* to me, something given. Thanks, Mom, thanks Dad, thanks God. We don't invent ourselves. We are given to ourselves. God didn't consult with you whether you wanted to exist. He wanted you. Because He loved you, and your possibility made him smile.

The Catholic faith community of this country has dedicated the month of October to the principle of the sanctity of human life from the womb to the moment of death. We've all seen those amazing pictures of a child in the mother's womb, that tiny little face yet to take their first breath…that child is you! We were all there at one point, in our entirety. Smaller? Of course. But that is *you*—all of you. Please be aware of all the respect-life issues that affect children (the right to be born, the right to food, clothing, and shelter, the right to education, work, and health care). Respect life means to be equally concerned with the poor, sick, and elderly. Watch how our candidates describe their plans to help life in all its stages.

A note to young people: working to secure these life-enhancing concerns is a great way to spend your life. Young people! Consider these matters as possible careers worthy of your time and talents. God bless you, and together let us work for a society that treats every person as a child of God.

Be in peace. God's got his plan.

Young People Are Amazing…and Goofy

The work of a parish priest gives one the chance to observe people in many different life situations.

The elderly smile and shine with pride when their children and grandchildren are home visiting. The steely determination of parents as they sacrifice for their children. Nervous newly engaged couples approaching the church to plan their wedding. A stay-in-the-hospital tends to bring out anyone's true colors. We priests see it all. But the ones that touch me the most are our young children and teens. They're so "out there," so new and raw, so…wonderfully goofy. Let's marvel for a moment at our young ones.

Doesn't it kill you when…

- They smile that kid's smile. It's radiant without their knowing it. The smile doesn't have the slightest notion of what we know (that heartache isn't too far down the road). "Oh," we say, "if only they could stay here." So beautiful.
- A young person shows off some talent or favorite activity getting friends or family to smile and applaud.
- The girls break into singing the current youth "anthem" at a party or game. They're so free in that happy way.
- The boys consume unbelievable amounts of spaghetti and get hungry twenty minutes later.
- The whole school turns out for a prayer service for one of their sick classmates.
- They try putting on some idea of adult behavior just to see how it feels.
- They collapse in tears and fall into your arms…and still want you near them.
- After days of whining and selfishness, they come out of themselves and do something amazingly thoughtful for someone. *Yay! It's working"* parents think for a moment. And don't you wish you could…you know…control their lives!
- Spare them the hurt you know life eventually hands out?
- Let them see what you see in them (how wonderful they are)?
- Give them the confidence they need without them having to earn it through trial and error?

- Choose their friends?
- Spare them bad, impulsive choices?
- Find the perfect job, boyfriend, girlfriend, roommate?
- Get them to experience God's Spirit working in their life?
- Ensure their happiness and safety throughout their lives?

Oh, how we want to live their lives for them! So the question for parents and grandparents is this: Do you think God loves these children less than you? He made them! He loved them so much, He gave each of them an unrepeatable personality, style, and soul. To top it off… God gave them *you*. So what's your part in their life now? Here they are, physically grown and old enough to make their own choices. So many choices out there; so many voices calling them to follow. They need you to witness to your belief in the goodness of life. They need you to show them why you continue to hope in spite of trouble and darkness…why you pray, why you believe in the goodness of people. Why you follow Christ.

Jesus may have been thinking of teenagers when he said, "Watch the wildflowers grow…they neither spin nor worry…yet not even King Solomon is as beautiful as these. Won't God be sure to watch over you?" (Luke 12:27–28). *But!* Teach these young ones to "Seek *first* my will in their life," says the Lord. "And these other things will come to pass."

What's God's part? "Take courage," he says. "I have overcome the world."

God is with you. Trust Him.

Divorced and Single Parents

Last week, we looked at life as a single person, never married, having no children. I felt I had something to say about it because I'm single. What I failed to communicate is that God plans this for some of us. He created some of us in such a way that we are happiest when living single lives. It's a *vocation*. A *calling from God* to bring Christ into the world in the ways described.

But what about divorcees and single parents? Did God change His mind and suddenly want these former spouses to live singly? Of course not. What changed was that one or both of the spouses were no longer able to continue living as husband and wife. Of course, this was not the way they intended things to turn out. If it were possible with a wave of a hand to fix their marriages, they would wave it in a second. Presto! All better.

We all know there is no magic to fix our broken relationships. How they break is sometimes simple but most times complex. People stop being loving. They stop seeking the happiness of their spouse, or they stop letting their spouse help them to be happy. It's messy and complicated, and usually, there is plenty of blame to go all around. In the midst of all this, it is crucial to remember that your current life is not some "plan B" (because plan A didn't work out). In the aftermath of marriage, many feel damaged or inadequate. Somehow, they failed to be what they were supposed to be, and now they must live life in some mournful isolation. And guess what? They observe, "I deserve it!" No! You are God's child, beloved by the Lord. You are Christ's presence to your children and family. You are absolutely crucial to the well-being of many people. They depend on you, they love you… and… God's plan is not done yet. You have a critical role to play in the lives of people you haven't even met yet!

Your vocation is right in front of you. It is to be parent to your children. No one can do that role like you. No one. God has personally given you this role with your children. They have your eyes, your nose, your temperament! You are their guide for life. How godly is that role! But can I ever marry again? Do I have to live a single vocation if I don't feel "called" to it? The prospect of remarriage is in one sense out of your hands. It depends in large part on another person (one who you love and who returns your love with theirs).

We don't order these things up on eBay. People come into our lives by virtue of how we live. The best advice I've heard for people in this situation is to live your life doing what is your duty—at work, at home, with family and friends…and then…to tell God what your heart longs for. Might God have prepared a future spouse for you? Quite possibly, but let it happen in God's time, in God's way.

"And Mary said to the Angel… Let it be done unto me as you Lord say."

Blessings to everybody. No exceptions.

When We Hate

It's scary sometimes how deeply we can feel anger or resentment toward someone or some situation. I'm not talking about being "annoyed" or "frustrated." No, this goes deeper. It surprises us with how hot it gets us; our reactions can be so strong that we say or do something that has devastating effects, sometimes for years.

Try this one out—did this ever happen in your family? It did in mine. I was a teenager (I'm guessing thirteen or fourteen years old). I can't even remember the issue now (some minor "no" to something I wanted to do), but I remember the flash of intense anger I felt and the words I spoke to my mother. "I hate you!" I said. "I wish I had a different mother!" (I'm feeling the shame of those words as I type this.) My mother, of course, being the adult and knowing her son could be a spiteful boy, walked away from this awful moment (perhaps to cry).

I look back on this incident some fifty years ago and wonder how my parents didn't put me up for sale! How can anger be so strong? How does it completely overwhelm our reason and better instincts? I don't know. It just does. It may go back millennia to the fury we needed to survive in the hostile environment of the animal wilderness.

What I do know is…it is *not* God's will that we act that way. Rather, "Get rid of all bitterness, passion and anger, no more hateful feelings. Instead, be kind and tenderhearted to one another, and forgive one another" (Ephesians 4:31). This is exactly what my mother did. And in doing this selfless act of parenting, she saved her son. Years later, I would recall that moment to her and how her sad but silent walking away showed how much she loved me.

I tell this story because I know some families who have allowed words (thoughtlessly spoken) to become a giant divide between parent and child or brothers or sisters. For some, it has been years since family members have spoken to each other. As I say, it's frightening how one moment of heated exchange can cost a lifelong friendship, or worse, a brother or sister or parent.

This same toxic anger is afflicting our political conversation. Both sides are infected, Democrats and Republicans. Each sees the opposing side as not just wrong or "misguided," but they are seen rather as the enemy whose heart is wicked and whose intentions are cruel. So long as we see our opponents as lacking character or moral goodness, there is little hope we can work to solve our common problems.

New effort must be constantly put forth to repair or renew tattered relationships—no matter how many times it takes. This is hard work and requires a basic trust in our neighbor's goodness. Where do we get the will to start again with that "stupid Democrat" or "blind Republican" or "foulmouthed child"? It comes in knowing that, despite present appearances (!), this is a child of God. Christ shed his blood for them and for me.

So as scripture tells us, we now have peace through the blood of Christ. "With his own body (Christ) broke down the wall that kept them enemies" (Eph. 2:14). In other words, he died for us all. If he refuses no one his redeeming love, can we?

Lord, help us turn the other cheek. It is your beloved child who strikes us.

"Wives Be Submissive"

Every year we hear this passage from Ephesians, "Wives be submissive to your husbands," and so this Sunday, we hear it again. Let the eye-rolling begin! Of course, it is immediately written off by many as a message from a different time. Today, we moderns see things in terms of "equality" and have freed ourselves from the old-fashioned roles of husband and wife. "Submission" feels like we're losers in some contest of wills.

Rather than spending time explaining what this passage does *not* mean (blind obedience and the self-effacement of women), let's look briefly at what this means *for husbands*. God's word is laying a burden on men that is different from the burden women carry. St. Paul calls them "the head" of family. What could this mean but to serve the needs of the body (of which he is a part)? To be a "look out" for those most dear to him…his family.

Every family needs someone whose major responsibility is to be watchful for dangers, observant of needs, and dedicated to providing a stable, safe, and peaceful home base (who goes downstairs in the middle of the night to find out what that noise was). The head. But can't wives do that just as well? Yes. Many do. Heroic single mothers are everywhere. They carry the man's burden as well as their own. I bet if you asked them if they'd like the man to carry his burden with her…and for her, she'd say, "Finally. Some help!"

C. S. Lewis writes, "It is painful, being a man, to have to assert privilege or the burden which Christianity lays upon my own sex. I am crushingly aware how inadequate most of us are to fill this place" (*God in the Dock.* p. 261).

He goes on to say we men often make very bad husbands (priests!). "That is because we are insufficiently masculine." Masculine in the way that is modeled in Jesus Christ. And that's the key for both husband and wife—to be like Christ for each other. Husbands, remember when Jesus spoke of himself as the good shepherd? "I am the good shepherd. A good shepherd lays down his life for the sheep… I will lay my life down for the sheep. No one takes it from me, but I lay it down on my own" (John 10:18).

Wives, remember when Jesus spoke to his Father in the garden the night before his crucifixion? Knowing that somehow his death would be the way his Father revealed the salvation of humanity, yet feeling the terror of what lay ahead—he submitted. "Father take this cup from me, but not what I will, but what you will" (Mark 14:36). Jesus was submissive.

And in the end, don't we all "submit"? Don't we give in to the wishes of those we love? Love wants to say "yes" every time! But love also knows it must be guided by what is right and virtuous. And here we are back again to the role of husband and wife. I hope we can still say clearly that the woman's heart pulls together the family relationships, giving that warmth and comfort that is her genius.

The man, if he's carrying his proper burden, has her and the children as his chief concern in life. He's the "lookout" for all of them. Protecting, providing, and yes, sometimes correcting. It's like a dance. You need a Fred in his top hat, and a Ginger in her flowing gown, joined in their coordinated whirl of love.

CHAPTER 6

Power of Prayer

Why Should I Pray?

In writing this column on prayer, I was looking over my books in hopes of finding some quote or insight that would help describe what prayer is all about. Rather than a description of "how to pray" or "forms of prayer," let's begin with a "reason to pray."

Praying is one of those things we know we "ought" to do. It's a good thing; it keeps our toe in the door with God. It is somewhere in the order of calling home to Mom and Dad on Sundays out of obligation and always something I was glad I did when it was over. So saying a prayer is universally recognized as a good thing to do; prayer is just one more good thing we just don't get around to doing.

So why should I pray? I mean it. Give me a good reason why I should pray. Otherwise, I've got hundreds of things to spend my time on which will bring real, tangible benefits to me and my family—like money, recreation, entertainment, etc. Some saint, I'm sure, would tell me to pray because it's the right thing to do; it gives proper praise to God who is "all worthy." Somehow, that just doesn't move me at this starting point.

Okay. God takes us where we are. Why should I pray? Because it will keep me from getting lost. Do you know what I mean by "lost"? Lost happens when the things we took for granted about life disappear…alone in life, no one to live for, no purpose to anything

I might do, no reason to get up in the morning, overwhelmed by life's circumstances, no hope for me or my family or the nation or the world.

How does prayer change this situation? It addresses the hunger of the human heart. It puts us in touch with who we were made to be—lovers. Lovers of God and this world. The human being was made for the express purpose and privilege of loving. Anything less than that diminishes us as humans. We become merely consumers, or professionals, or hobbyists, or sports fans.

But what if my heart doesn't hunger for anything? That's a problem. "Blessed are those who hunger and thirst for righteousness," says the Lord. But "Woe to you who are satisfied, you will go hungry" (Luke 6:25). The problem is our hearts are set on the things that do not satisfy our deepest human needs. Prayer sets us on the path of finding the heart's desire.

Now these are just words about prayer. Why it's good to pray. They are not prayer. You discover prayer by praying.

At Home with Yourself

W. B. Yeats called it the ever "widening gyre" ("The Second Coming"). The image was of a falcon and the falconer who calls the bird to its roost. The bird has flown to a distance, it can no longer see or hear its master. "The falcon cannot hear the falconer. Things fall apart. The center cannot hold." The poem refers to the forces of history or culture that take a person and a civilization away from their true self.

Something like this happens in every age. Its effects appear in our culture today, and our young people are most severely affected. We're losing a sense of our center, our true selves, and what is most disconcerting—we don't sense the loss. The forces that separate falcon from falconer are many and complex. To keep it simple, we can point to an imbalance of the "inner world" and the "external world."

The inner world refers to that awareness a person has of himself. His center. His loves and hates, personality characteristics and values. It's our soul, our center. It's the "me" that tells me it's time for bed at night. The "outer world" of course is that environment outside ourselves: events, relationships, whatever grabs our attention during the day.

Between these two poles, my human life happens. I go out of myself to encounter the world, then I return to the inner world, and the conversation with myself begins. "What was that? Why did that happen? What do I need to do now?" etc. These two poles of life, the going out and the returning "home," need to be in balance. The problem is the world, with the unending chatter of social media, news and entertainment, overwhelms the "inner person." There's no home to return to. A certain anxiousness can happen. Things fall apart.

Ever have one of those moments when television, the phone, or Internet are all turned off? We grow restless or slightly embarrassed to be "alone with ourselves" (COVID sequestering did this to many of us). The sudden quiet catches us off guard. In the silence, a weird feeling of being a stranger to ourselves comes over us. And so we check our e-mail, text someone, see what's on TV, phone somebody…anything to avoid being with oneself. This estrangement from ourselves has sad consequences for our relationship with God. How can we hear the voice of God if we can't hear the voice of our own conscience (that inner voice rewarding our good action or calling us to account for bad).

Remember Jesus telling us "when you talk to God (pray) go to your room. Close the door. And pray to your Father in secret" (Mt. 6:5–6)? Why in secret? Because God doesn't want to share you. He wants just *you*…your inner self. Here you can give your full attention to the visiting Spirit of God. "Speak, Lord, your servant is listening" (1 Samuel 3:9).

Remember musak? It was that bland, person-less music that played familiar tunes in elevators. It was invented to keep us calm as we waited with others for our floor. You never thought to ask, "What is that song they're playing?" because it was meant to be in the background. "I heard it…but I wasn't listening." So listen to your heart. It's full of things you've wanted to tell God. "Lord, it's me. I just want to tell you…" Many times, it's just being aware of your feeling and giving them to God "who sees."

So how to end this? Get quiet. (Five minutes is a good start.) Put down the iPhone. Come home to yourself. Reacquaint yourself to what you're feeling, thinking, loving, fearing. Then…turn to Him. Speak anything (anything!) you want to get off your chest. (The Holy Spirit will quietly guide your prayer.) He is there. "Your Father who hears in secret…knows what you need" (Mt. 6:8).

That is a promise from Christ. Trust Him.

Praying Like an Adult. How to Start.

Not to sound overly dramatic, but I don't see how any human being can stay faithful to a life promise (marriage, priesthood, doctor, president, pope) without at some time "saying a prayer."

I think of my priesthood. Oh, I could have stayed a priest without praying, I guess. The perks are pretty good (free room and board, heated garage, pretty vestments). But without prayer, over time you become a shell of a priest, just going through the motions.

Husbands and wives, you know this too; anyone who tries to commit themselves to a project or a promise sooner or later runs out of gas. The promise you made way back now seems impossible, or perhaps in your frustration, it appears "unimportant." "Why should I spend any more sweat and tears on this darned thing that never seems to get any better?" Been there?

So why is prayer the answer to being "out of gas"? Because it reconnects us to the source of love and faithfulness… God. It takes us out of our empty, exhausted, defeated selves, and lets us become children again. It lets us experience our neediness without embarrassment. Prayer calls out to God, who Himself has promised to watch over and help us in our times of trouble and emptiness. "Come to me," Jesus said. "All you who are weary and heavy burdened, and I will give you rest" (Mt. 11:28). "Pour out your hearts to the Lord" (Psalm 62). "Your Father in heaven knows your need, even before you ask" (Mt. 6:8).

So it's been a long time. I've been away from my childhood religion. I feel like I'm lost in a forest, how do I start praying like an adult? Do I rattle off a couple of Our Fathers and Hail Marys? Okay. That's a start. But there is so much more.

Here are a couple of thoughts that will help get you started.

- Gratitude is a wonderful way to get you in the right attitude for praying. No matter what your current mood may be, there are some things in your life that "you just know" (for example, I know my mother loved me. I know my father's advice about hard work has proved itself time and again). And I know in the same way there was a time that God answered my prayer, *or* at least I'm aware He has blessed me with a gift I could never even imagined by myself. Even on a crummy day, this thought lifts my spirit. Gratitude. It works every time.
- Once you're feeling a little gratitude, it leads to a moment of trust. "You've helped me in the past, Lord. So I turn to you now, please." Trust that He will catch you as He has in your past.
- Finally, there's the little matter of surrender. Remember Jesus in the garden? His whole world was collapsing. What was his prayer (after telling God his own wishes)? "Not my will, but yours (God) be done."

All this points to prayer as a moment of personal speaking to God who "sees (and hears) you in secret" (Mt. 6:6). It ought not to rattle on with fancy or churchy words (when the building is burning "fire!" is all you have to say).

Just speak from your heart, "Thank you, Lord, for the time when…" "Dear God, you know what happened, please help me…" *Or* just… "Help, Lord."

- Now just sit a minute. Don't do anything. Like you're on your porch listening to the evening breeze. Look out your window, whatever.

- Lastly. Pay attention to the conversations and events of the week. They often contain God's surprising answer to our prayers.

This brief conversation with God needs to happen every day or as often as you can make it happen. If you do this for a while, you will begin to experience in wonderfully vague way (!) God's presence with you.

Eight Things About Prayer

Life is busy, hectic, and messy. Sometimes, important things, like prayer, can take a back seat. If you need help jump-starting your communication with God, here are some helpful hints to start again, and perhaps help make this time more effective. Take some time with each of these:

1. The very thought or desire to pray is an invitation from God.

    No one can say "Jesus is Lord" (1 Cor. 12:13) without a grace from God. So every time your heart is lifted, however faintly, it is God actually reaching out to you. Let this be an encouragement. God loves you and wants your friendship. He begins the conversation.

2. Prayer is about friendship and trust in God.

    So how do friends speak and listen to each other? Honestly, straightforward, without fear of offending, knowing your friend cares for you.

    Warm up to prayer. Don't just jump in the pool. Take a minute or two to "prepare" your meeting with God. You're beginning a holy moment. Best practice: it takes about ten minutes to shake off the noise of the world and get down to business with God.

    A memory is a good start. How has God helped you in the past? At the beginning of your prayer, thank Him for that. It helps to get a memory bank of times God has intervened.

3. Bring a "prayer starter" with you. Read over the book of Psalms. Pick out three or four psalms that speak to you. Bookmark them and turn to one of them after you've settled yourself. Quietly and slowly read the part that touches you. Pause and read it again. Then sit patiently, let your thoughts come and know you've given them to God.

4. Start where you "are," not where you "should be."

This is very important. You don't "get holy" and then start to pray. We start right where we are. Lazy, selfish, angry, happy…whatever. Give yourself to God just the way you are. That's what friends do. But remember… He's the Lord. His will is the path to life. End your prayer by submitting to God's will, just as Jesus did in the garden.

5. Again, "holy" thoughts are not what God wants. God wants *you*! In all your imperfections and failures. He'll begin to show you a new path, but it starts right where you are! Find *your* way of praying, not someone else's.

6. We learn to pray by praying, and remember the Holy Spirit will help you. You are not in this alone.

No one ever learned to play the piano by reading about it or seeing a video. You learn by putting fingers to the keys. So too with praying…just do it. There's no one there to grade you. God will take whatever you offer him and magnify it. Remember the mustard seed (Mt. 4:31)?

7. Be quiet. No thoughts. Just look out your window. God is with you.

After you've read scripture and spoken to the Lord, it's time to listen. God speaks to us with thoughts, memories, and sentiments that move our will to want what God wants. Oftentimes, it's only later in the day (or week!) we realize what God has done in our prayer.

8. Don't try too hard. God comes in quiet peaceful moments, oftentimes unnoticed, like a bird landing quietly on a branch.

    Just know that the smallest of gestures toward God brings His blessing. God loves you. You are his child. Keep on trusting, keep on asking, and keep on looking for signs of his hand. "Seek and you shall find" (Mt. 7:7).

Prayer. Just do it. It's what love does.

Praying: A Simple Start-Up

Ok, get rid of all your pictures of "praying." The bowed head, the folded hands, the gaze heavenward…forget them. That's for holy cards. Your prayer must be *yours*.

Below you will find some important things to "know about" prayer and then some hints about "how" to pray (what to do).

1. Prayer. God starts it. Any thought like "Gee, I should pray for that," OR "I need to go to God with this problem," that's God! He's giving you a grace! (an invitation to pray).
2. Which child gets the most attention from a parent? The one who struggles with things, right? Don't worry about your prayer looking pretty. Trust God to know what you mean. The Holy Spirit is working in you.
3. Prayer is "wanting." Wanting goodness, wanting peace, wanting happiness and then turning to God who is the source of all this.
4. Quiet is really important to prayer. Get quiet. (I like to close my eyes.)
5. It takes a minute or two for the "noise of the world" to flow away (this, too, is prayer).
6. Speak what you want to bring to God briefly and honestly.
7. Having an "image" of God can help but is not necessary. God is in your brain seeing and hearing everything you are!

8. Was my prayer a good one or a bad one? Bad question. Any prayer is a good prayer.

How to pray for three minutes each day:

1. Make the sign of the cross. Take thirty seconds to be quiet. (No words. Nothing.) Let the world settle around you. Trust that God is watching with you.
2. Now say His name in your mind, "Lord" or "Jesus," "Holy Spirit" or "Dear God." Let His name echo in you for another thirty seconds (say His name two or three times).
3. Next, tell God how things are. (One minute.) Are you carrying a heavy burden? Worried about something? Has there been a blessing in your life to be thankful for? Speak these to God as you would to your best friend. Remember, tell God your feelings ("how you are"), not what you need (solutions).
4. You're there now…praying! One minute to go… After you've told God how it is for you, be quiet again. Relax and know God heard every word you just gave Him. The Lord will many times send a feeling of "peace" at this time (thirty seconds).
5. Finish with a request for the day. Something like "Help me today, Lord, I need…" Close with an Our Father and/or a Hail Mary.
6. This is just the start. God will teach you more each time you come to Him in prayer. We learn how to pray—by praying!

Keep up your hope. God is working in you.

Store-bought or Homemade?

I really don't think most of us have much of an understanding of what prayer is and how to do it. Of course, we know the prayers we learned by heart as children. The Our Father, Hail Mary, Glory

Be…what else? Angel of God, My Guardian Dear, Grace before Meals, Act of Contrition. That's about it.

So prayer at this level might be described as "words we've learned to say to God." And this is a good thing. Sometimes we need prayers already made up for us. They help us when…we hurt too much to use our own words; we need a quick prayer for a quick need; we just don't know what to say to God.

I like to use the image of cookies. What's your favorite? I like Oatmeal Raisin. There's a particular brand I buy at the store. (I can eat half of them at a sitting!) But we all know nothing compares to homemade cookies. We put ourselves into them. Our hands, our ingredients, our time, our senses are all involved! I made these cookies. "Store-bought" or "homemade," they're both good, but sometimes nothing will do but the ones you make yourself. It's like that with prayer; someone else's words may fit our prayer most of the times, but every once in a while, I need some homemade prayers.

That's the kind of praying I'd like to be better at. I'd like to really talk to God. And I want to hear God talk to me. I don't think that's too much to ask. So how shall we do this? Why not get together and read what Jesus told us about prayer (scripture), and then hear a little talk about praying, and then…pray! As our teachers used to tell us, "You learn the piano by playing the piano." We learn how to pray by praying.

In the meantime, I'd like you to be thinking about the following questions just to get you revved up a bit. No "store-bought" answers here, what do *you* think about these?

- Name the times you pray in the course of one week.
- What do you do when you pray?
- How do you know when you've prayed well?
- Did you pray as a child? How?
- Do you enjoy prayer?
- How would you describe the Holy Spirit?

- Does God answer prayers? How?
- Do you like to pray alone or with others?
- On a scale of 1 to 10, how much do you want to be a better "prayer"?

CHAPTER 7

Finding Hope: "Dealing with Temptation, Addiction, and Failure"

Hope

There is a scene in Lewis Carroll's *Alice in Wonderland* where Alice eats a mushroom and grows to enormous proportions. She outgrows her bed and bedroom. She must get on her knees so as not to hit her head on the ceiling. Her arms get stretched out the windows. She doesn't fit in her world anymore. It's too small for her.

Silly as it sounds, that image keeps coming to me as we think about the great mystery of Christ's resurrection. This world is too small to fit our hope. Here's what I mean. Prior to Christ being raised up to the life of the resurrection, this world was all we knew. You were born. You grew up and did a bunch of things (it really didn't matter what you did). And you died. Everything was all part of the giant wheel of life. Spring to summer, summer to fall, fall to winter, and then it starts all over again.

We all fit in to the ever-repeating pattern of nature—birth to death. Like a giant Etcha Sketch, nature would lift the page, and our scribblings would be lost...forever. The best we could hope for was a good growing season, a healthy baby, a little comfort in our last years.

The best prescientific minds reflected this static, never-changing universe. The sky was thought to be a giant dome (think Sky Dome in New Orleans). The stars were stuck into the dome-like spotlights. Each day, the biggest light, the sun, followed a path etched in the dome. As the book of Ecclesiastes tells us, "What has been, that will be; what has been done that will be done. There is nothing new under the sun" (Ecclesiastes 1:9).

That all changed when God sent his son into nature (space and time). Jesus, by virtue of who he is (God in human flesh), removed the dome over the earth and opened the night sky to the infinite reaches of the galaxies. No longer are we humans caught on the mindless, ever-turning wheel of life. No longer are we like leaves that bloom in spring and return to the earth each autumn.

We are children of God. God, who Jesus tells us to call "Father." We now have reason to hope for a life that unites us to God forever in Jesus Christ. Without this hope, we're stuck in Alice's tiny house. "If for this life only we have hoped in Christ…we are the most pitiable of people" (1 Cor. 15:19). Christ has freed us from the eternal return that held us captive and so now "we look forward to the Resurrection of the Dead and the life of the world to come." The creed.

Still, we live in time. There's not enough, it seems. We run out of it. We come to our end. Jesus died; so do we. This fact has not changed. But…as the women at the tomb tell us today, *He is risen!* God is not defeated by death. He lives in eternal life. And He's coming to get you. Christ wants us to be with him. Why? Because he loves us. Why does He love us? Because that's how God is.

Oh Lord, increase my faith. Please say "yes" to Christ's love.

Ulysses and the Sirens

There's this scene in Homer's *Odyssey* where the boat of our adventurer Ulysses comes near to the island of the Sirens. He tells his men to tie him fast to the mast of the ship so that hearing the Sirens' seductive song, he will be unable to fling himself into the sea toward them.

Dangerous rocks lay all about the island, and to come too near meant certain shipwreck. It's a great story (written three thousand years ago). We call it Greek mythology. Did it happen in actual history? No. It's a myth. But is it true? Of course, it's true. Is there a "song" that if you listen to it, you'll be tempted to abandon your ship? You bet. Just ask the alcoholic whose friends invite him to a bar for "a couple of cold ones." Ask the teenager (hormones raging) who knows of a website where "you can see it all." Imagine the hoarder who hears about "buy one, get one free."

We all hear the Sirens' call. They know just the song to sing to each of us to have us sail toward that rocky shore. So what do we do? (We're talking about temptation, of course.) The first thing to do is be aware of the power of temptation. It has the uncanny ability to get under or around our desire to do the right thing. It needs to be respected for what it can talk us into. Be smart. Know how strong temptation can be.

Next thing. Be prepared. Know where you want to go. Know where you don't want to go. Before the Sirens start "your song," be like Ulysses: take measures that will help you resist. You don't have to tie yourself to a mast (!), but do something to help you resist.

- Let your friends know in advance that "you can't go there."
- Use your computer in the living room where others gather.
- Let a trusted friend know what your temptation is and ask their help (if only to listen to you and encourage you to keep up the good fight). Ulysses asked his crew to tie him up!
- Pray daily for help to resist the Sirens' song. God will come to your aid. St. Paul says if all else fails, your resolve is gone: "God is faithful and will not let you be tried beyond your strength: but with the trial he will also provide a way out" (1 Cor. 10:13). (The Spirit gives you a good idea to do in that moment.)
- Lastly…*run away!* Fleeing is a great way to defeat the Siren's song. It's not weakness to run. It's wisdom. Someone yells, "Fire!" It's not cowardice to flee!

Actually, Ulysses was pretty lucky. He could have messed up big time. You see, he had his men put wax in their ears so they wouldn't even hear the Sirens. He, however, had heard how entrancing their song was, and he wanted to hear it for himself. So no wax for him! "I want to hear them sing." (It's called the "near occasion of sin." Don't go there.)

Lucky, the mast held him back, and he returned to tell his amazing story.

We humans......how patient God is with us.

Hope: How to Give It

Most of us look on the word *hope* as referring to a feeling that somehow things will turn out happily (I hope it's sunny for the picnic. I hope the Yankees win the World Series. I hope I don't get sick.) This common kind of "wishing" has nothing to do with Christian hope. These "hopes" serve more as a barometer of what my bodily wants are at this particular moment. I hope for what I want.

Christian hope is different. It is an expectation that our life here on earth is for some purpose. And that purpose, though we can't see it yet, will somehow be realized. What makes it a different kind of hope is that it is given to us by God. It's not something humans could ever have thought up. It's beyond any reasonable human expectation. It comes from God who had this in mind when he made us.

So where does this hope come from? It comes from the love of God revealed in the death of Christ for us. "This hope does not disappoint for the love of God has been poured out into our hearts through the Holy Spirit that has been given to us. God proves his love for us in that while we were still sinners Christ died for us...now justified by his blood...will we be saved by his life" (Romans 5:1–5, 8). Jesus, according to St. Paul, has unlocked a door to God we never knew existed. "Through Christ we have gained access to this grace (God's love) in which we stand, and we boast in hope of the glory of God" (v. 2).

Why is our hope a certainty? Because it's based on the love of God "poured out" into us. The promised hope all hangs on Jesus's death on the cross. It is there God, if you will, proves his love for us. Darkness and evil did their worst on Jesus. They killed him. But (and here's our hope), Jesus was raised from the dead.

So how do we give this hope to our children?

* First of all, *God* wants to give it to them! The Holy Spirit is constantly "poured out" on them in moments of happiness, challenge, goodness, sorrow, etc. Trust that. Tell your children, "Watch for God today, he's going to whisper to you."
* Parents/grandparents, you are the biggest giver of hope to your children. How you live on a weekly basis, the hope you exhibit in your conversation, your positive response to society's problems, your prayers at dinner and before bed…all are moments your children watch to see if you have hope.
* Share your burdens as an adult (in an appropriate way, of course). Ask for their prayers about a particular intention. This gets the children involved in real faith situations. Plus, they want to "help" Mom and Dad.
* Don't shy away from hard situations involving suffering. Someone you know is sick. Pray for them. Someone has died. The older children might go to the wake with you (you decide when they are ready). Let them know that Jesus himself died so we didn't have to be afraid—because we are going to God.
* Maybe you have to do a little work on yourself. Perhaps you need to ask God to help you with those human situations that cause you fear or worry.
* In all things, just know that God has given you your children just as they are. He will help you teach them the way of hope. Don't be afraid.

Lastly, hear the words of St. Paul as he was held in prison, facing death for witnessing to Jesus Christ, "What will separate us from the love of Christ? Will anguish, or distress, or persecution, or…peril or the sword?… For I am convinced that neither death, nor life, nor angels, nor powers, nor present things, nor future things, nor any other creature will be able to separate us from the love of God in Christ Jesus our Lord" (Romans 8:35–39).

What makes us so sure? Jesus Christ is risen from the dead!

Addiction: Part 1

"These things are addictive," he said as he finished the bag of honey-roasted peanuts. We all know what that means in an everyday sort of way. There's something that tastes so good, is so easily available to eat, and repeats itself with each mouthful that's it's hard to resist eating too much of it. But in the common mind, it doesn't qualify as a real addiction until we experience an inability to stop. It becomes a way of acting to which we are driven (even in spite of our better judgment). Where does this strange power over us begin?

St. Thomas Aquinas would tell us it begins with something quite good: stimulation, comfort, ecstasy, release, approval. Many earthly activities bring about these enjoyable psychological states—food, drink, sex, winning, etc. The "pleasure" attached to these activities is there to ensure their repetition. Food is delightful to the taste because nature wants to ensure we eat every day. Sex brings intense pleasure because nature must find a sure way to foster new generations. They are strong inducements to these particular actions, but by themselves, they are not necessarily addictive.

What makes a particular thing addictive is its power to ever increase the desire for such a state over other human experiences. There comes a point where to *not* be in that state is experienced as a deprivation, a sort of poverty. I begin now to prefer my addiction to all the other states of being. I seek to always increase the time I might spend with it.

At this point, the addictive power begins to limit human freedom. (Master and slave is not too strong in comparing the addict to his addiction.) There is no end to my desiring this activity. It will not quietly take its place amongst other human activities. Like the moon which disappears at sunrise, the other good things of life can't compete with the blinding desire of addiction.

Moments like kindness, friendship, generosities, humor, communication, as good and pleasurable as they are, are not addictive because they lack the power to overwhelm. One experiences these moments without others losing their comparable appeal. They are psychological states freely chosen amongst other human offerings. Their appeal does not remove other choices, even some less pleasurable.

Where does the addiction get its power? Science has been hard at work to unwrap the phenomena of addiction. They tell us over time the repeated brain waves of intense pleasurable action wears a pathway in our brain. Along this frequently used brain path travels powerful pleasure-inducing hormones (pheromones) producing the increasingly desired effect. In effect, the brain has found a shortcut to the feeling of "well-being." It's only a matter of time that this easy "wellness" becomes the preferred state from which to engage the world. All addiction is, in a sense, a drug addiction (the pheromone release in my brain.)

Other addictive theories are more behavior based. But they, too, have a "pain relief" purpose. Psychologists tell us we all have elements of emotional pain in our lives. Some pain is lifelong and comes from traumatic instances in our youth. Others, less dramatic but chronic (loneliness, depression, fears, boredom, etc.), can turn to certain behaviors that self-medicate painful emotional states. For example, a person tied to a job she hates, without family or friends to enjoy life with, with little or no hope for anything changing for the better, can self-medicate at the casino, the bar, the Internet, the kitchen, etc., anything to change the low emotional wellness level.

Let's be honest. We all run the risk of finding something to which we are inclined in an unhealthy, addictive way. Feeling his weak human nature, St. Paul writes to the Romans, "My inner being delights in the law of God. But in my body I see a different law. A law that fights against the law of God… I don't understand what I do; for I don't do what I want to do, but instead I do what I hate. What an unhappy man I am! Who will rescue me from this body that is taking me to death?" (Romans 7:14–25).

The answer, of course, is God. But we need to understand what we must do so God can do His part.

Addiction: Part 2

Let's begin this reflection with a promise given to us by God. "For I am convinced…that neither death nor life, neither angels nor other heavenly rulers or powers, neither the present nor the future, neither the world above or the world below, there is nothing in all creation that will ever be able to separate us from the love of God which is ours through Christ Jesus our Lord" (Romans 8:38).

That said, the power of addiction will be overcome by God's grace. Period. God does not want His children in bondage. So we need to find a way to let the power of the love of God into this dark and scary place. How do we do that? It's probably best to turn to those who have experienced a release from their addiction. The first people that come to mind are our brothers and sisters in the twelve-step program of recovery. Over the years, they have discovered a certain path to victory over addiction to food, alcohol, pornography, gambling, etc. These twelve steps, if followed with docility and humility, will lead to freedom from addiction.

I want to focus on the first three steps, as I feel they hold the key to all that follows:

Step 1: We admitted we were powerless over _____.

Step 2: Came to believe that God (my Higher Power) could restore us.

Step 3: Made a decision to turn our will and our lives to the care of God.

Here I think is the genius of the twelve steps. It comes by admitting we've lost the battle. The addiction is just too big and too strong to hold out against. Every time it is me vs. my addiction… I lose. How do I know that? Because I've tried a thousand times to *not* do that, and a thousand times I failed. So the key to "sobriety," as they say, is to admit I've lost. It's a moment of terrible honesty with oneself when we admit "I can't control this. It controls me." This takes real humility. Our enemy the devil sows seeds of protest in our mind. "No," we say, "I could stop if I really tried. I'm not a loser here."

That is a lie. Here's the terrible truth. I have lost the battle. It's over. I'll never overcome this addiction. We have to give up trying to fix this by ourselves. Because we can't. So…now what? Just give up and give in? Of course not! Something very positive has just happened. We've admitted the truth—"we can't." There is no shame in this. It's just the way it is.

But now comes the positive side, something you can do. Steps 2 and 3 point to a moment when "we came to believe that God will help" and "we made a decision to turn our will and life over to the care of God." (I have to emphasize that this "came to believe… God" is totally blind and without a foothold. It's like bungie jumping into the Grand Canyon…at midnight.) He's there. Trust the promise. It's like saying, "I can't, God. But you can…if I get out of the way." Then the daily repetition of these steps begins (sometimes out loud to God in prayer). "I can't, Lord. You can. I'm yours. Do what you want with me." Daily…daily…we have to return to these steps: surrender, believe in that power beyond yours, and giving Him charge of your life.

Slowly, sometimes quickly, the compulsion to engage your addiction weakens. It doesn't go without a fight, however. It uses many tricks and voices in your head to try to convince you how futile are your efforts. "You'll never lick this. Think how boring and cold life will be without me to comfort you. You'll never make it without me (your addiction)." All lies.

So much more to consider on this topic, but for now I think we focus on two things:

1. "I surrender… I've lost the battle."
2. "I'm in your hands, Lord. I'll be the clay; you are the potter." You will begin to see God's freedom dawn on you.
3. Don't give in to discouragement. You are a child of God. Always.

CHAPTER 8

Storytelling

A Cocktail Conversation

I had a conversation the other day with a bright, accomplished businessperson. Business was not his only pursuit; he has written books on grief and counseling (something he'd become quite an expert at). He's retired and devotes his time to helping others. This is one of the good guys.

So he started talking about the "human spirit" and how everyone has a divine spark in them to guide and enlighten. I nodded agreement, though I'd have chosen different words. (It was a cocktail conversation—you know those!) What surprised me was his conclusion about the "human spark" we agreed we all have. "We're each responsible for what we do with that spiritual gift." On one level, I totally agree with my friend. Our life is in our hands—to make of them what we will. This is the dignity and responsibility of each of us. Every life has this chance to define them. But are we all on an even playing field as we start our "journey to become"? Do we all have an equal chance at the good things of life? Do some of us get a head start that helps us achieve success? I think we do. Let me explain.

Consider what we need to succeed in life. First of all, we need a set of values that guide our actions: honesty, perseverance, respect, hard work, etc., right? And where do we get those values? At home, of course, from our parents. Secondly, we need proper education at school. The cognitive skills we develop (reasoning, communicating, problem-solving) combined with knowledge of technology lead to opportunity in life and in the marketplace. That being achieved, you're ready to make your life's story.

But what if those two critical elements (home and education) were lacking in your upbringing? What if your young life was marked by poverty, or a broken home, or frequent violence? What if there was no one to model behaviors of honesty and hard work? How would you have turned out?

I think of my father, who, seeing his son so careless in my schoolwork, set himself directly in my path, saying, "Your schoolwork comes first, *then* sports. *Do you understand, Tim?*" "Yes, Dad." I hated the thought of not playing basketball, but there was only one way to make that happen. I had to study. My old man was there to ensure that happened.

You get my point, right? Without the guideposts of family and the values of education, I'd hate to think of the bad habits and choices I would have made. By myself, I'd probably have a reserved seat at some bar in town. Now some might respond, "Well, I've worked hard for what I've got. No one handed it to me." Good for you! Really, congratulations. *But* could you have achieved your life without help from the very beginning? There are some who have overcome huge obstacles to reach a life that contributes to society. We call them heroes…or saints. There are many. But many more have found themselves overwhelmed by a "cycle of poverty."

So how can we help? I think it begins by recognizing the blessing we've had in our early lives and felt a compassion for those who, for whatever reason, have not had these many helping hands. Then we can begin to speak up for the disadvantaged, look for ways to ensure compassionate government and law enforcement…and, when circumstances permit, speak to our neighbors about helping the social disparity so many experience.

After all…in the end, it's all a gift.

"Bless Me, Father, for I Have…"

Two weeks ago, I and three other priests had the privilege of listening to some sixty fourth graders confess their sins to Jesus. It was really very touching. It's times like these that I feel I share something of what you mothers and fathers feel toward your children at times of sorrow and contrition—nothing but tenderness.

One by one they entered the confessional. Some were eager, smiling, almost like a visit to Santa, they couldn't wait to tell their sins. Others, perhaps a bit more thoughtful, came somewhat shyly. Their faces were furrowed a bit at the brow (I believe these were among the first of the tens of thousands of furrows that will mark their faces one day as parents themselves). These children knew what they had done wrong, and it was a concern to them. Their innocence and genuine sorrow for their sins was so touching, I had to resist the urge of stopping everything to hug them.

After the words of absolution, with their sins forgiven, there was a lightness that happened in them and in me. We both would smile, and there was that exquisite feeling that comes when you know God is smiling at you. And off they went to kiss Mom and Dad. Now there's something that makes me sad here. The children stop coming to this fountain of forgiveness. Like all children—they forget what happened that day. And they don't come to confession again for a long time (maybe not until the week of their marriage—when the priest reminds them of the sacrament of reconciliation).

Do you want to know the number one reason children don't go to confession (or mass on Sunday for that matter)? Because the parents don't make it a priority. And why don't the parents go to confession? Because they have no sins? Help me out here! Friends, *we have forgotten the sadness of our sins and the joy of God's mercy*. There is a whole lot more to explore here. For now, I would just like to remind us of the invitation we have from the Lord to *leave the past in ashes*. What a powerful image this is of what can happen to our habits of sin when we come to the fountain of forgiveness that is the sacrament of reconciliation!

God loves you so much. Please let Him show you by forgiving your sins.

God in the Mess

Part of our training to become priests was to experience real life trauma in people's lives. The thought is to get the man out of the pulpit and sanctuary and put him in a situation that is seriously out of control. See how this fellow handles tears and tragedy…can he still be a positive agent for the faith? Can he help people whose life has just been crushed with tragic circumstances?

So off we went for a summer. We were chaplains for hospitals, jails, psych wards; others to first responder chaplaincies (police, fire, EMT). I traveled to Dallas, Texas, to Parkland Memorial Hospital, an excellent eight-hundred-bed county hospital. One of the duties of the new chaplain was to be on-call over the weekends. (Basically, you were called in on any human upset the head nurse thought necessary.) All kinds of stuff happened, especially with a full moon.

One memorable night brought the death of an elderly, long-suffering grandmother. Though quite poor, she had raised a large family, and they in turn were busy raising families of their own. They'd all been keeping vigil as the grand lady weakened daily. About three in the morning, I was called to the waiting room to help the family deal with Grammie's death. Children and grandchildren were all there. The room was jammed. Thirty people, I'm guessing. Just as I'd feared, they were going nuts. Screaming and crying, "Oh, Grammie, how could you leave us?" The men were the worst. I remember one fellow in cowboy hat and boots on his hands and knees banging his head on the wall. Others were pulling at their hair (I'd never seen that before).

So what do you do? Fear and panic filled the room. One person's cries caused others to howl. They were freaking out. This ship was sinking fast. I really can't say I said a prayer—I just went with my gut. "Be quiet!" I yelled as loud as I could. Two or three times… "Be quiet!" Finally, the howling stopped, and these big tough cowboys were all looking at me (I had no idea what should come next). *God help me,* I thought. Then came His grace. Somehow, I thought… *Give them something to do.* But what? "Men, comfort the women." (As I said, the women were doing pretty much okay. But it got the cowboys out of themselves for that moment.) In a flash, everybody was hugging someone. Sanity came slowly back.

And that, friends, was a moment of grace far away from the pulpit and the altar. It was God in the here and now. God in the mess.

Have you experienced Him there? In a difficult moment with your spouse? Your child's meltdown? Some unexpected incident? Bad news about a friend or loved one?

How does God help? Generally, I think God gives us something "to do." Something really simple, like…say something (don't say "be quiet!"). How about… "I'm so sorry," "You must feel terrible," "Do you mind if I sit with you?" Or perhaps just to listen, to touch (when appropriate). Just something to break the awful tension of the moment—your gentle voice can heal in the simplest of ways. Be that safe place for someone.

So what's your situation? Married? Children? Student? Single? Sad? Feeling blessed? Need money? Worried?

Whatever and wherever you find yourself—there is God's Spirit. This present moment.

We can wish we were somewhere else. Perhaps it was our thoughtlessness or selfishness that got us where we are. In the end, it doesn't matter. What matters is "right now." God is with you.

Don't be afraid.

Serve Somebody

I hope by now you know how happy I am being a priest. I've told many young men that, were I given the opportunity to choose my life over again, I'd be a priest. I just like it. It fits me. Perhaps the biggest reason it feels right is that I think God wanted me to be a priest. It was His idea first…and then ever respectful of my freedom, God found ways to get me thinking about this way of life. It makes me happy to think God has an opinion about what we should do with our lives.

He never forced me with fear or guilt. God used natural human things to get my attention…comments of people who knew me well, watching some priests who I liked a lot (seeing their happiness and humor), feeling a desire to help people, the staggering beauty of the world, realizing that we're only here in this world for a while…all contributed to a growing feeling that God was calling me to live my life as a priest.

It wasn't easy to hear God's voice calling. It requires listening in prayer, a careful examination of your heart and its feelings, and hardest of all was trying to find "my heart's desire." In the end, it came down to the Lord asking, "Tim, who will you give it all to?" And the answer—though it took a while—was "I want to give it all to you, Jesus. I want to be so filled up with you that all I want is to "be yours" (I'm guessing this is how brides feel on their wedding day). "And then, Jesus, I want to share you with people and do the things that will help people get to heaven." For me, that said "be a priest."

That's my story in four paragraphs! It certainly wasn't my mother and father's story. It's probably not your story either. Most people don't have that odd appeal toward a celibate life lived for the purpose of spreading Christ's kingdom. I mean, really, let's face it, it's pretty different.

But…your story and my story have that most important aspect in common, "Who will you die for?" Or, to put it in a milder way, what is there in your life that you would be willing to sacrifice it all for? That's God's invitation to you. That's your vocation. For my father, it was a beautiful woman named Rosemary. For Mom, it was her husband and her children. And they did. They laid it down for each other and for us children.

And do you know who in the end we all lay it down for? Teacher, parent, spouse, priest, musician, poet, carpenter, farmer, soldier, cop, nurse, bus driver…we are all called to lay it down for Christ. Yes, that's right, you have a vocation to give your life to Christ, to be at His service each day of your life. The only problem is we don't see him. Know why we don't see Him? Because He's hiding! He's hiding in the face of your spouse, your students, customers, friends, enemies, your children, your parents, your neighbor, your checkout person, and yes, even the guy who cut you off in traffic! Yes, all humankind is united to Christ in the moment of the Incarnation and now in the Resurrection.

You get it, right? "Whoever wishes to save his life will lose it, but whoever loses his life for my sake and that of the gospel will save it" (Mk. 8:35). We are the only creature made by God that comes to understand their life by giving it away. That's all of our vocations—to lay it down in love. "Anyone who has given so much as a cup of cold water to one of these little ones…will not go without reward" (Mt 10:42).

Jesus and My Mom

St. Paul tells us we are "Ambassadors of Christ. It is as if God were appealing through us" (2 Cor. 5:20). On this Mother's Day weekend, I'd like to give you an example of someone who was an ambassador of Christ for me. God working through a person to get to me. It was my mom.

I was in my third year of seminary studies (with two more to go), and I had gotten to the point of wondering if I'd made a mistake thinking I could do the things a priest must do. Studies were getting quite demanding, and my formation board was pushing me to manifest a more "generous spirit in the community." I was getting pretty grumpy.

On a short visit home, with Dad taking a nap upstairs, my mother and I had a little visit in the living room…just the two of us. I asked how things were with Dad and her alone in the house. How was she feeling? Then she asked about me; how seminary was going. Most times, I would put the best version forward. ("Great, Mom. Everything's just fine.") But this time was different. I told her how hard it had been and how I wondered if I could ever do all the things they expected of me. It all came pouring out…the long days, the difficult professors, the high expectations. "Mom, I just don't know if I'm the guy they want. I don't seem to fit the mold."

Now you'd have to know my mother Rosemary to understand how unexpected was her response. You see, my mother is not what you'd call the nurturing type. She was a brilliant conversationalist with a charming personality (Lauren Bacall would play her well). She preferred the company of adults to children. A martini and a good story was where my mother thrived. So you can imagine my surprise when this elegant woman, with brow furrowed, said, "Well, you might not be right for *them*...but *Jesus* wants you, Tim. You're going to make a fine priest."

The words at the moment were touching. My mother just doesn't talk like that. Here was a mother loving her son. I felt better. Cocktail hour followed immediately! But the "God part" followed the next day as I drove back to Rochester. Somewhere along that boring drive, I began to replay my visit and the conversation with Mom was soon recalled. I felt again the warmth of her words, her unquestioning confidence in me, and her faith that Christ would use her son to be a good priest if that was His will. At this point...and I can't explain how...my mother's words "you're going to make a fine priest" were heard as if Jesus were speaking them. It was my mother's voice I was recalling, but it was Christ who was speaking to me there in the car.

Jesus used my mother's words to give me the confidence that God wanted me to continue. My heart was light and happy as I drove back to the seminary that day.

You are an ambassador of Christ. God appealing through you. Be ready. And bless you mothers...you gave us life. And then you show us Christ.

Lord, Help Me to See

I think I was around twelve years old when Mom and Dad took our family on one of our rare family vacations. We went to Monmouth Cave in Southern Kentucky. It is a magnificent cavern deep, deep in the ground filled with stalactites and stalagmites with beautiful crystalline gems flashing brilliant colors.

There are many memories I have of this trip. One which sticks out the most, and one that still speaks to me fifty years later, is the sight of a school of brown trout swimming in an underground stream that flowed through the cave. Generations of these fish had lived on the floor of this darkened cave—dark as in pitch-black.

The park service had installed lights along a portion of the underground stream allowing visitors a brief glimpse of the fish who otherwise lived in total darkness. Over time something very strange had happened; with absolutely no light penetrating the cave, these fish had lost their eyes. How strange it was to see that milky white membrane over what should have been a dark round fish eye. Over the generations of darkness, nature had seen the futility of sight and basically closed up shop. Use 'em or lose 'em!

You see, of course, the analogy to faith here, right? Faith is a way of seeing how God is present and acting in the world and my life. When we were children, it was easy to see God's handiwork. Remember?…snowflakes (not one of them the same), the stars at night, the ocean, thunderstorms, babies, kittens, flowers, ice cream, clean sheets, stories at bedtime, Christmas eve, strong parental arms around them…all these wonderful experiences lead a child to know there is a God (most times through you, but sometimes from the Holy Spirit himself). A child is a lover of God by nature. It's what they do. ("Unless you receive the Kingdom of Heaven like a little child you shall not enter" [Lk 18:17]).

But then…well, you know. We grow up; get "real." We see and hear things that shake us, changing the way we view the world. Along with this, we discover a part of ourselves that can do bad things. We look around and see a world that doesn't pause when we stumble and fall. Good people we've known have fallen prey to lies and tricks and been changed in the process…they've "toughened up." And God sort of disappears. We can't see him for the darkness around us. In fact, like the fish, we can lose the eyes to see. The sentiment of faith becomes a distant childhood memory of our first communion or setting up the nativity scene. We've let darkness put a membrane over our eyes.

So what do we do? Why not do what the blind man did in Luke's gospel? "He called out, 'Jesus, have pity on me!'" (Lk. 18:35ff). And Jesus asked him, "What do you want me to do for you?" The blind man answered, "Lord, I want to see again." To which Jesus replied, "See again! Your faith has saved you."

It's really that simple. Acknowledge the fact that you're blind to the things of God. You can't see anything but the world and its cynical message—"Good luck, pal."

The next step can sometimes feel like falling off a cliff. When, from the center of your being, you gag forth the words, "Lord, I want to see again." Lord, help me see you in my life and in my wife and in my work and in my child and in my trials and…and…and."

God cannot resist this prayer. In time—persist! You will hear the Lord, "See again."

Let this open your eyes to see God's presence in your life.

On Call (A Story for Priests)

Two or three times a month, each priest on the east side of Rochester are on call at Rochester General Hospital. Eight in the morning to eight the next morning, we respond to any calls for the anointing of the sick or the sacrament of confession. Sometimes I forget I'm on call. This was one of those nights…

So it was Sunday night about nine fifteen. I'd just settled in to watch the closing ceremonies for the Rio Olympics. The chaplain at Rochester General calls to ask for an anointing. A woman, ninety-three, in a coma…her son was asking for a priest. So you go, right? Of course. It's what we do. On the way, I try to spiritualize my frustration at missing the Olympics. "Lord, this is for you. I offer this up. Let this bring me closer to you and your sacred heart." I silently patted myself on the back for responding quickly and calmly to the chaplain's request. "I'm a dutiful priest," I tell myself.

Her name was Ruth. She was curled up in a semifetal position. With eyes closed, her head was tilted back as if expecting a knock at the window. Tom, her son, greeted me with a kindly smile and extended his hand. He told me his mother had come to the hospital with a lung infection, but I soon learned this was simply the last in a litany of health problems that went back decades, back to when Tom and his sister were told their mother had Alzheimer's, and special care would be needed for her 24-7.

For twenty-two years, they watched their mother's growing dementia as Tom cared for her in his home. It had been years since Ruth even recognized him as her son. "We just wanted to be ready, Father. She's been through so much." Briefly he fills me in on what the recent past had been and the numerous trips to emergency rooms. I was struck by the tender way he spoke of his mother and the total absence of any reference to what these years had cost him and his sister. (It set me thinking of my sisters who each cared for our mom and dad in their final days. Like little children, our sickly parents needed constant care and attention which both of my sisters gave so readily.)

And here he was, bent over his mother's bed stroking her hair. I wondered if I was kind enough, generous enough, selfless enough, to do what this man had done for so many years for his dying mother. Suddenly, my frustration over missing the Olympic closing seemed so small and petty. My prayer of "offering up" seemed less heroic, and my secret estimate of myself suddenly paled when compared to Tom's undivided devotion.

So what's my point? We've all been witness in our priesthood to persons of great charity and holiness. For me, the people I hold to be in the state of great sanctity (who knows these things?)…most are simple everyday people…few are priests. The point is we priests have it pretty easy. The great love of God's people for the priest paves the way for a smooth landing in so many life situations.

Most people do the hard, thankless, everyday carrying of their burden with no fanfare. We priests hear "thank you, Father" almost daily. Most people get gifts on their birthday; we often get little candies on our desk "for just being you." Most people pay for their meal; how many times has someone across the restaurant picked up Father's check? Their moods don't get pampered like Father's when he's "having a bad day." So I guess I'm urging us priests to see ourselves as Jesus did, "It is the same with you; when you have done all you have been told to do, say, 'We are but servants; we have only done our duty'" (Lk. 17:10).

We priests stand humbled by the hidden souls whose brilliant charity daily sow the seeds of God's kingdom.

Feral Dogs

The thought came to me this week hearing St. Paul's exhortation, "We no longer live for ourselves. While we live we are the Lord's and when we die we are the Lord's. Whether we live or die, we are the Lord's" (14:8). See what you think of this. We seem to have developed a renewed love and fascination for dogs over the past few years. Certainly, you've seen the television ads where the family dog sits with everybody on the couch watching TV. Or the adorable puppy that cuddles with its owner and plays with the children on the carpet. Our hearts are touched.

But did you know that millions of dogs run wild in this world? They gather in packs to raid livestock and threaten humans when approached. They're called "feral" or wild dogs. There are no rules in their pack—food and breeding are what drives a feral dog. You wouldn't want one on your couch.

What make them wild? They lack a master. Someone to teach them to live with humans. Someone to demand certain behaviors that make them loving pets for owner and children. And when trained, they experience a dogs' life that is the envy of any wild dog.

Got the picture? It's a bit of a stretch, I know, but the same thing applies to us humans. St. Paul says we have a master. It is the Lord. We were created by God unlike any other creature. We weren't made to sit on His lap, or lick His face; no, ours is a far greater privilege—we were made to be God's children. To live in His Kingdom. To love and be loved as persons. Through Christ's humanity, we now actually share in God's divinity.

But here's the rub. We need a master. Someone who knows more about us than we do. Someone who sets the rules for our well-being. Someone who becomes a rule for our life. Without that, we become feral. Many will say, "We have our science and technology to improve our life. We have our reason to solve problems. We have the rule of law to govern us. We are our own master." Yes, but *who* created us with these powers? And is there no one to whom we are responsible for how we use them? Our brilliance learned to split the atom. Yes, and now there is a source of unlimited power. But this same knowledge enabled us to make the atom bomb. Human genius invented the Internet (yay!), but now we have those dark places that are only two clicks away. Oh dear. We have unlocked the human genome, and now we have the power to clone human life. Who is our master? No one. We become "intelligent animals." Feral humans.

Please don't think I disparage the amazing advancement science and civilization have made in human history. (Psalm 8 says it so beautifully, "What are humans that you care for them…yet you have made them little less that a god. You have given them rule over the works of your hands. Put all things under their feet.")

This is all great news about us humans—so long as we recognize God as our master. And what kind of master is our God? Some stern and joyless king? Some faceless power that set the laws of nature and now sits back to judge? No. It is the Lord Jesus Christ. He died that we might know God's love for us. And once we know the love of God…we can bend our knee and cry out … "My Master!"

Bless you. Child of God.

A Parable: The Twenty-Dollar Bill

Deacon John Juneau at the Cathedral Parish told me this story. I think it's a great example of a modern-day parable. After reading this, see if you can summarize its meaning in a single sentence.

A famous professor, known for her ability to engage her students, began the lecture one day by holding up a new crisp $20 bill. "Anyone who would like this piece of paper, raise your hand." All hands went up.

Next she crinkled the twenty into a little ball. "Who wants this piece of paper now?" Again, all hands were raised. Unfolding the wadded twenty, she wiped it across the chalkboard. "Still want this?" All hands rose. On she went, grinding it with her shoe, slamming the door on it, finally dunking it into her morning coffee. "Who wants this now?" Everyone raised their hands wanting to get this filthy, soaking, ragged $20 bill.

Two questions:

1. So what's the meaning? Try saying it in one sentence.
2. Do you see any lesson it might have for human beings?

Here are my sentences:

1. It's not just a piece of paper; it's a twenty-dollar bill!
2. Battered, stepped on, filthy, it doesn't matter; we never forfeit the sacred value we have as being human beings, created in God's image.

What's in Your Memory Box?

Years ago, there was a home visit in the parish I'll never forget. I was bringing holy communion to a couple in their eighties. The husband was bedridden, so we said our prayers bedside, and they took the host. Afterward, the missus invited me to their overheated living room to "chat a bit." A huge gray cat eyed me from the corner. Some minutes into our first-time introductions, she asked me, "Do you want to see my braid?" "Excuse me?" I said. "My braid, I've saved my hair."

So what does one say? "Sure. Let me see your braid." In a flash, she sets a handsome mahogany box on the table. Lined in red velvet, the box contained what looked like a thick dark brown rope about the size of a braided garden hose. It was the hair of a young woman. Her mother had insisted that scissors not touch her hair from birth to her eighteenth birthday. This box contained the beautiful hair of her youth. She smiled remembering how she looked with that beautiful auburn hair.

What is my point? There are some things we should never let go. Some things are so precious that they continue to feed us, inspire us, touch us long after the actual event. We talked last week about scars and the painful memories they can bring and how God can use them to bring about character and compassion for others. So too, we each have unforgettable memories that make us smile, that warm our hearts, that make us proud. God gives these to us as our very own treasure chest.

He wants us to open it often and remember the wonderful work He let us be a part of. Why? So that we become aware of the goodness of God in our life! So that we can "connect the dots" and find God present to us in the people and events of our life.

So what's in your treasure chest?

Mine? Here's a couple of mine:

- Our screened-in porch and garden growing up.
- My dad reading the newspaper at night in his chair.
- Senior year basketball. Beating Gilmore Academy in triple overtime.
- A moonlit walk with a first love. Fifty years ago. (Pretty corny, eh?)
- My sweet sisters constantly forgiving me for my unkindness.
- A tree where God sat me down and let me know He was with me.
- Friends who love me and still talk to me after many years!
- The grace to walk away from a harmful habit.
- Some genuinely holy people who have graced my life.

All these cause me pause to remember God's invisible hand guiding me in my life.

Your homework? Think back. Find your moments and…give Him thanks.

PS: Remember, God is not done with you yet. Keep your eyes open.

Youth Takes Courage

The readings this Sunday remind me once again of a time long ago when youth had to face the challenge of growing up. Isaiah sees the glory of God and draws back. Peter sees the power of Christ's invitation and wants to escape, but in both cases, they were given a moment of strengthening, the power to trust that the risk they were about to take would be protected by God. Ah youth!

When God made young people, he put huge amounts of hormones in them to make them brave, passionate, risk takers (without that, I wonder if we'd ever move out of our parents' home). We wonder why we can't have guarantees in life; why is life such a risk? Because if everything turned out just the way we wanted, love would wither and die. We'd *expect* success to any effort we make…that wouldn't be love. Love has to give itself away. No promise of payback.

Every couple has that moment of risk: (a romantic setting, a ring, "Will you?" "Yes!" and later on… "Shall we?"… "Shall we what?"… "Shall we have a baby?" "Of course! Why do you think I bought the roses?") "Love believes all things, hopes all things" (Cor: 13).

Below you'll find my "risk moment" in becoming a priest. I've written about it before, but it still speaks to me. It happened forty-six years ago.

A grain of wheat. What is it but a little package of life? In it is contained all that is needed for a new plant, or tree, or wildflower. But something has to happen for it to become what it was made to be. It has to die. Unless it dies, Jesus says rather plaintively, "It remains just a grain of wheat." As if to say "what good is that? A seed that won't die."

We are like a seed, a package of Christ's life given to us at baptism. And like Christ, we must die to ourselves like a seed in the ground. I'd like to share a moment when God made this crystal-clear for me in a very personal way. It was late August of my twenty-sixth year. I was renting the upper half of a house owned by a nice widowed woman. I had been teaching high school the past two years and after much struggle was accepted into the seminary for studies for the priesthood. But now serious second thoughts were occurring as school was a week away. "What were you thinking?" I asked myself. "Do you really want to do this?" I was all knotted up.

To help clear my head, I offered my landlady to clean the gutters of leaves on the second-floor roof. Climbing out my window onto the roof, I had a lovely view of the street and garden just below.

Looking down I saw all these little green oak tree sprouts growing just under the gutter. The acorns had rolled off the roof and onto the ground, and there they grew. All but one acorn…it had fallen into the gutter and sat for who knows how long. It was big and round and still had its little acorn hat. *What a smart little acorn you are,* I thought. *Staying nice and safe in this gutter. You didn't die like your little brother and sisters down below.*

So with my thumb, I pried the little cap off the acorn to look inside. And there it was, filling the entire acorn with its bright orange body…a giant maggot. It had eaten the entire inside of the acorn. No green little oak leaves sprouting up from the ground, this acorn was now home to a giant worm.

I threw the acorn to the ground, and not a minute later, the Holy Spirit whispered to my heart, "But if it dies, it bears much fruit." Unlike that hesitant acorn, I came down off that roof and planted myself in the seminary…where I had to die about ten times before becoming a priest! Those little oak trees would be forty-five years old by now.

Message to youth—pray about it—if it's still there in your heart—do it!

CHAPTER 9

Joy and Love

All I Know Is That I Was Blind and Now I See

These were the words of that wonderful little man in the gospel. He had been born blind and from his earliest days lived a life as a beggar. (I remember in my hometown a man sitting on a busy corner, a hat and sunglasses covering his face, selling "Blind Man Pencils.") Everyone in town knew him. You would think it was a cause for great joy that this poor man was given sight for the first time in his life. But not for the keepers of religious propriety, "Whoever healed you is not of God, for this was done on the Sabbath…this man is a sinner" (John 9:2).

What's happening here? The man is being bullied. He's being pushed into a theological debate that he is sure to lose. He's dealing with the experts in the law, and they're mounting a powerful case against Jesus using the most forceful argument of all…it's against the law to heal on the Sabbath! So what does he do? He refuses to be drawn into their academic game, and instead he witnesses to what he knows is the truth. "I don't know if he is a sinner or not. All I know is, I was blind and now I see."

Ever have that kind of bullying? You know, the "professors" in the lunchroom / locker room, "Oh come on, you don't have to go to mass to talk to God. Besides, they're all hypocrites anyway." Or "You Catholics are such prudes, you love to feel guilty." Or "Those people just don't want to work. It's in their blood. Why should I have to help them?"

What do you do? I like the little guy's lead in. "All I know is…" In other words, he doesn't get tangled up in someone else's conclusions. He doesn't debate them on their carefully prepared arguments. No, he simply states what he knows to be true. He stands to witness for something that is unpopular to the experts, the majority, the current opinion.

It's not easy, is it? The man is thrown out of the synagogue for telling the unpopular truth. People shun the messenger of inconvenient facts. Dietrich Bonhoeffer, the Lutheran theologian who died in the Belsen prison camp, describes this as "the cost of discipleship." It's part of the program that goes with following Christ. People won't understand you, will try to shout you down.

So…what is it that you know? We don't have to look too far. Life delivers lessons every day.

For example, I know:

- God helps when we call out to Him.
- Kindness is its own reward.
- Spreading hope is what we're about, not pointing out failure.
- Everyone, everyone, is a child of God.
- Somehow it's going to all work out (because God has saved us).

So go witness to "all I know is…"

Falling in Love

This week, I thought to write about something younger people are concerned with…like…falling in love. (Share this with your children or grandchildren.) When you think of the human experiences that most change and motivate our lives, falling in love has to be right near the top. I've seen selfish, sullen, sarcastic twenty-two-year-old men suddenly become thoughtful, generous, and gentle. The reason? They met someone to love.

It's a fantastic feeling, isn't it? To think that someone who makes me weak in the knees whenever they are near…actually feels the same way about *me!* "Finally," we say, "I've met the person just meant for me! They make me feel so good."

Been there? Lucky you.

What causes these powerful feelings in us? In no small part, it's hormones. Our bodies are speaking to us. Telling us we need to be thinking about finding someone to continue the human species. This profound emotional swelling is meant to help us fulfill one of the purposes of life—children, family, home. This is how God made us. These feelings are holy, ultimately to be shared with the one who will be a partner for life.

But then…like a summer's day, the feelings can change. Life has other things that have to be dealt with: work, finances, life goals, etc. The thrill of first love becomes a steady, everyday, sometimes, boring "presence" to each other. Young lovers can sometimes feel their hearts have tricked them. "He/She is not as exciting as they used to be."

I've been with young married couples who feel they've "fallen out of love." Perhaps this *is not* the one meant for me. Maybe we made a mistake. It can be scary. If a couple has been honest with themselves and each other along the way, what is happening is quite normal. God is leading them to a deeper experience of love. Though sex appeal and passion will always have great value, something deeper is happening—if they let it.

The lovers are beginning to experience the essence of love… self-sacrifice. The concern is no longer "how she/he makes me feel." Love is now learning to seek first the happiness of the beloved. The partner's happiness becomes the happiness for the one who loves. It's no longer about you. It's about the beloved. Here is where some can't deal with the switch. When I'm not getting the same feelings, I must not be in love, they think. Some abandon ship.

So permit this old man to suggest a few clues that tell you you're truly in love.

- You're basically happy when you're around that person (not ecstatic, just happy).
- You admire and respect that person more than most of your friends.

- You feel honored to be loved and respected by them.
- Even if that person would never meet you (if you could only watch them from afar), you would still find them lovable without their loving you.
- You're transparent with them because they are your dear friend.
- You know they would be a good mother/father.
- You know they are not the perfect person, nor will they bring you total happiness…and that's okay.
- You're willing to stop comparing him/her to others. They're the one.
- You've seen him/her in difficult situations, and they have reacted with kindness.
- A kiss on the cheek from them always brings comfort in the storm.

Lastly. The person described above is a *gift*, not someone you can order up by wanting it. And if by chance God doesn't give you this gift, He's got something else just as good for you…because he made you and loves you.

Scars Can Heal

I'm told that if you travel to Elmira and stand at the main downtown intersection, you will see a line on a limestone building (up about fifteen feet) that marks the level the floodwater reached in the flood of 1972. All you need do to remember that terrible event is look up on the side of that building. Scars. They serve as reminders of events long past. I had a broken front tooth served up by my sister swinging a bucket of water (sorry, Patty!). We all have physical reminders of bumps, scrapes, and collisions (mothers have reminders of their pregnancies). They don't hurt anymore, but they bring the event back to memory.

You know where I'm going with this, right? Yes, there are emotional scars too. Sometimes a place or picture or person can bring back an event that we can still feel (a couple of swimming episodes in my youth still cause anxiety whenever I'm in water over my head). There are, of course, "good scars," unforgettable moments of joy or peace.

Some of those emotional scars go deep into the psyche and subconscious mind. They create vague, hard-to-explain motives for our reactions to things. Counselors, psychologists, and spiritual directors help us locate "our issues." Things like: authority, intimacy, commitment, trust, addictions can all be affected by emotional scars. So what are we to do with these "visitors from the past"? Wise spiritual counsel says to be aware of them. "Know your demons." Facing these things honestly, sometimes with the help of trained professionals, can keep them from immobilizing us.

Christian faith assures us that we are not "defined" by our scars. In other words, what we are is given to us by God and will never be taken away. Our ultimate purpose as children of God is to receive the love of God (eternal life) and to know and love God in return. There is no scar, no fear, no devil that can rob us of this dignity. Parents, you especially understand this in your love for your children. Wherever they may be…at home, at work, in hospital, in jail, wherever…they are always your child. Even in hell (God forbid), I would be God's son.

So what does this mean for scarred, addicted, fearful humanity? It means that *nothing* can change what God wants for me as his child. In fact, our very wounds can become the thing that God uses to show us His love (I've heard people tell me their sickness/addiction is the very thing God used to touch their hearts). St. Paul says it beautifully (I quote at length):

> We know that all things (even our scars) work for the good for those who love God and who are called according to his purpose… If God is for us who can be against us? What will separate us from the love of Christ? Anguish? Distress? Persecution? Peril?
>
> No! In all these things we conquer through him who loved us. For I am convinced that nei-

ther death, nor life, nor angels, or principalities, nor present things (scars!), nor future things… nor any other creature will be able to separate us from the love of God in Christ Jesus our Lord. (Romans 8:28–39)

So what does this mean when my demon memories come calling? It means I don't have to run and hide. It means I have that scar, no denying it. It means I am more than what has afflicted me. But what has scarred me can, by God's grace, help others to bear theirs. "Peace be with you," Jesus said. "Then he showed them his hands and his side. The disciples rejoiced" (Luke 24:40).

Love bears all things. Love never fails.

Smile

Sometime ago, I lived and worked with an old retired pastor. He was revered as a priest who knew his parishioners and had that "golden touch" with people who were troubled or lost. People flocked to him to receive his gentle wisdom. He had one particular habit however that bugged me. At the end of every mass he celebrated on Sunday, he'd tell the congregation, "Be sure to share your smile." It was his sign off. People waited for these last words from him.

As for me, I thought how "corny" it was. It was just too simple. I mean, for all the problems we face, for all the worries we have for the coming week, for all the problems of the world…all you can say is "Share your smile"?

But you know what? He's right. Share your smile is brilliant. Why? Because it sends a universal message. Everyone knows what a smile means. *Webster* defines it as "a favorable, pleasing, or agreeable appearance; characterized by an upward curving of the corners of the mouth." And what does this "upward curving of the mouth" say? It says, "You're worth it. You are not invisible. You're a fellow human being and I'm sending you my good wishes."

It can literally change a person's day. Suddenly, someone has seen me and cares enough to offer me a tiny "be well." A smile disarms us of our fears, touches us briefly with kindness, and becomes a light in the midst of gray and shadow.

Some people have that gift in spades. They have a wonderful smile. I remember a seminarian who sometimes worried whether he had the pastoral skills needed but who had something the rest of the class lacked—he had a magical smile that brightened any room he walked into.

You just feel better when someone smiles at you, don't you? So why don't we do that more often? I think it's because (1) We're afraid. We're afraid of being "misinterpreted" or frowned upon or ignored. (2) We're self-absorbed. "I've got too many things on my mind right now. Too much to do. You stay in your lane; I'll stay in mine." And (3) We think we have an ugly smile. Forget it. A real smile is never ugly.

So how do we get over our fear and self-absorption in order to give the gift of a smile? Some thoughts:

- Your smile is a tiny gift, which any person is worthy to receive.
- Someone giving you a smile lifts your spirit, right? So do that for someone else.
- Giving a smile is an act of kindness and makes you a better person (and it often lifts the mood of the person smiling).
- It costs nothing.
- You're prettier when you smile.
- Don't care or expect it to be returned.
- The best dogs can do is wag their tail—only people can smile (so what's holding us back?).
- A smile softens everything. It takes the edge off clumsy words or awkward moments.

So I'm going to work on my smile this New Year. I'm not going to expect people to return it. After all, it's a gift. And should I forget, maybe your smile will remind me.

So I'll end this column like that old pastor… "Be sure to share your smile."

God's smile is upon you.

Wonder

I keep coming back to a human experience that I think holds the key to understanding who we are as a human species. It is the experience of "wonder."

Think of it, scientific knowledge, as wonderful as it is, is in the end "about things." Science tells me an apple is a red, yellow, or green sphere of cellulose, permeated with sugar and water; or ice cream, "a food consisting of cream, butter fat, sweetener and frozen." Does this *Webster Dictionary* description tell us what vanilla ice cream really is? Of course not. Human knowledge, to be more than stored computer facts, is experiential. You have to taste vanilla to understand it.

And here's where the "wonder" part comes in. The most important human experiences elude scientific description; we say things like "You have to see it for yourself." Some things (the Milky Way in the night sky, a newborn baby, the death of a lifelong friend, or my own mortality) present a moment that is beyond our ability to fully understand and leaves us in a state of shock and "wonder."

The psalms are full of this mysterious sense. "Oh Lord, how awesome is your name through all the earth! / You have set your majesty above the heavens! / When I see the heavens, the work of your hands / the moon and stars that you set in place /…how awesome is your name through all the earth!" (Psalm 8)

Psalm 139 echoes this same moment of wonder and awe… "Such knowledge is beyond me, too lofty for me to reach… How precious are your designs O God; how vast the sum of them. / Were I to count them, to finish I would need eternity."

Fear and reverence accompany such experiences. We meet face-to-face a truth that is real but beyond our ability to fully comprehend. It overwhelms us with its mysterious presence. Such a moment came to me at age nineteen. I had tickets to an outdoor summer concert by the Cleveland Symphony Orchestra. Its world renowned concert director, George Szell, had just died. There at midstage was placed the empty maestro's chair. Before some eight thousand rapt concert-goers, with the sun setting on a soft summer night, the orchestra (without conductor) played the soulful strains of Bach's *Air on a G*

String in his honor. Something happened to me, and I think to many in the crowd that night.

All I can say is I was overwhelmed by "beauty." And I mean beauty on a thousand different levels: The music, transcendent; the new grass, all around; the man (now gone) who created this magnificent orchestra, but still present as his musicians played; the thousands of people, silent and in rapt attention…and me, feeling nineteen, and ready to change the world.

It was a moment. We were all plugged into something that I can only describe as *joy*. Something bigger and sweeter and more powerful than any one of us. We were together, but each of us still ourselves. And we all "looked and saw how good it was." Can we say heaven was there for a moment? I can; at least, a hint of heaven. Quite simply, these moments are the foothills of God. Children waken to these hills every day. Everything is fresh and full of wonder. They hold that key to who we are…the creature that can know and love the Lord.

What's happened to us? Somehow we've lost the eyes to see and the ears to hear. We fill our senses with far lesser beauty. Our cell phones and computers, as wonderful inventions as they are, "reality TV" replaces real life with its wondrous joys and sorrows.

Is there a remedy? Of course, there is. Prayer.

Every day. "Lord I want to see your face, your presence."

He knows your need. Ask Him.

You're Special

It's human nature to want to be recognized, set apart, or seen as unique. We take great efforts to ensure this happens throughout our life, beginning with the very names we give to our children. Names are chosen to honor someone or something which has touched or inspired us in some way. With our special names, we set out to make our mark in the world. As kids, we decorate our bikes with streamers and flashing lights. We start to develop our own "style." The haircut we get, our favorite color, the shirt we like.

Certain music talks to us. Certain entertainers or sports figures become our heroes. We decorate our homes, lockers, offices all in such a way as to say "this is me" (the tattoo business is booming). Why do we do this? Because we are unique. No one has ever existed in earth like you. This is something to be celebrated! Parents, isn't this your goal with your children? To raise happy, confident young persons who know who they are and what gifts they bring to the world? Of course.

But we must be careful here. Our "specialness" comes from God making us in his image and from those who love us into life (parents, family, friends). To them we are special. As for the world…we're just one of what? Six billion human beings living on this earth.

My point is "being special" comes from being "good," from being loved. Everyone needs to be loved. Where things can go wrong is thinking the world owes me a life of fun and excitement and boundless opportunity…because "I'm special." I'm afraid we're raising children in such a way that when life deals disappointment and heartache (and it certainly does), when the world turns cold and cares less about how unique they are, our young ones feel like they've been tricked. "This is not the world you told me I was entitled to!" "This is hard. The world is not respecting me and my plans for life. Don't they know 'I'm special'?"

This is where unhappiness happens for millions of people in our country. Life just didn't turn out the way they thought. Somehow, it was all supposed to just happen. Happiness. No thought was given to how you deal with failure and disappointment. They had no concept of life as "struggle," no resource to deal with disappointment.

So what's a body to do? Several options are available.

1. Get bitter. Life stinks, and my mission in life, my contribution, is to let everyone know how unfair life is.
2. Blame someone or something else for your problems. It's the government, the school system, the coach, the current administration, the job market, etc.
3. Drop out. Just stop trying. What's the use? The world doesn't care that I'm special, so why should I try?

Parents, grandparents, here's how you can help. Teach your children that life is real and earnest. It's not a cakewalk. You will teach them everything they need to succeed, but only by their efforts will they carve a happy path through life.

Teach them that life is sometimes not fair. But here too you will give them all the recourses they need to stay on their feet. And what are those? "You are my child. God made you and gave you to us. And yes, you *are* special...to us."

ABOUT THE AUTHOR

   Father Timothy Horan (1948-2023) was a priest in the diocese of Rochester, New York. After serving faithfully as priest, pastor and friend in seven parishes for more than forty years, he passed away on July 4, 2023, Independence Day. His last assignment was as pastor at Holy Trinity Parish in Webster, New York.

   He had an ongoing devotion to helping young people open themselves to God's call and find their vocation in life. He served as director of vocation awareness in his diocese for thirteen years, guiding young men to the priesthood.

   Father Tim credited his father for instilling his faith, his mother for teaching him to see things that others missed, and the people of God who "always show me Christ's love in action.

Printed in the USA
CPSIA information can be obtained
at www.ICGtesting.com
JSHW021432191123
52347JS00003B/9